GUYANA

Marxist Regimes Series

Series editor: Bogdan Szajkowski,
Department of Sociology, University College,
Cardiff

Further Titles

GUYANA
Politics, Economics and Society

Beyond the Burnham Era

Henry B. Jeffrey and Colin Baber

Frances Pinter (Publishers), London

Lynne Rienner Publishers, Inc.
Boulder, Colorado

First published in Great Britain in 1986 by
Frances Pinter (Publishers) Limited
25 Floral Street, London WC2E 9DS

First published in the United States of America in 1986 by
Lynne Rienner Publishers, Inc.
948 North Street
Boulder, Colorado 80302

Printed in Great Britain

British Library Cataloguing in Publication Data
Baber, Colin
 The co-operative Republic of Guyana: politics,
 economics and society.—(Marxist regimes)
 1. Guyana—Social conditions
 I. Title   II. Jeffrey, Henry B.   III. Series
 988 '.103   HN330.3.A8

Library of Congress Cataloging-in-Publication Data
Baber, Colin
 Guyana: politics, economics, and society.
 (Marxist regimes series)
 Bibliography: p.
 Includes index.
 1. Guyana—Politics and government—1966–
2. Guyana—Economic conditions—1966–
classes—Guyana.   I. Jeffrey, Henry B.   II. Title.
III. Series.
JL689.A15B33   1986   988 '.103   84-62669

ISBN 0-86187-418-8
ISBN 0-86187-419-6 Pbk

ISBN 0-931477-23-9
ISBN 0-931477-24-7 (pbk.)

Typeset by Joshua Associates Limited, Oxford
Printed by SRP Ltd, Exeter

Editor's Preface

This, the first comprehensive book on Guyanese politics, economics and society, comes out at a time of renewed interest in the country's future. Forbes Burnham, who dominated Guyanese politics for the last two decades, died unexpectedly on 6 August 1985. He attempted a unique combination of Marxism and co-operativism. It is hoped that this book will allow the reader to judge the level of its success and the possibility of its application elsewhere.

Guyana is the only Marxist regime where an official parliamentary opposition is allowed. Interestingly, the opposition People's Progressive Party is also a Marxist party, led by one of the most prominent and respected Caribbean Marxists, Cheddi Jagan. This book is a timely, long overdue and much needed comprehensive study of the social, political and economic transformation of Guyana and the country's prospects in the post-Burnham era.

The study of Marxist regimes has for many years been equated with the study of communist political systems. There were several historical and methodological reasons for this.

For many years it was not difficult to distinguish the eight regimes in Eastern Europe and four in Asia which resoundingly claimed adherence to the tenets of Marxism and more particularly to their Soviet interpretation—Marxism–Leninism. These regimes, variously called 'People's Republic', 'People's Democratic Republic', or 'Democratic Republic', claimed to have derived their inspiration from the Soviet Union to which, indeed, in the overwhelming number of cases they owed their establishment.

To many scholars and analysts these regimes represented a multiplication of and geographical extension of the 'Soviet model' and consequently of the Soviet sphere of influence. Although there were clearly substantial similarities between the Soviet Union and the people's democracies, especially in the initial phases of their development, these were often overstressed at the expense of noticing the differences between these political systems.

It took a few years for scholars to realize that generalizing the particular, i.e. applying the Soviet experience to other states ruled by elites which claimed to be guided by 'scientific socialism', was not good enough. The relative simplicity of the assumption of a cohesive communist bloc was questioned after the expulsion of Yugoslavia from the Communist Information Bureau in 1948 and in particular after the workers' riots in Poznań in 1956 and the Hungarian revolution of the same year. By the mid-1960s, the totalitarian model of communist politics, which until then had been very much in force, began to crumble. As some of these regimes articulated demands for a distinctive path of socialist development, many specialists studying these systems began to notice that the cohesiveness of the communist bloc was less apparent than had been claimed before.

Also by the mid-1960s, in the newly independent African states 'democratic' multi-party states were turning into one-party states or military dictatorships, thus questioning the inherent superiority of liberal democracy, capitalism and the values that went with it. Scholars now began to ponder on the simple contrast between multi-party democracy and a one-party totalitarian rule that had satisfied an earlier generation.

More importantly, however, by the beginning of that decade Cuba had a revolution without Soviet help, a revolution which subsequently became to many political elites in the Third World not only an inspiration but a clear military, political and ideological example to follow. Apart from its romantic appeal, to many nationalist movements the Cuban revolution also demonstrated a novel way of conducting and winning a nationalist, anti-imperialist war and accepting Marxism as the state ideology without a vanguard communist party. The Cuban precedent was subsequently followed in one respect or another by scores of regimes in the Third World who used the adoption of 'scientific socialism' tied to the tradition of Marxist thought as a form of mobilization, legitimation or association with the prestigious symbols and powerful high-status regimes such as the Soviet Union, China, Cuba and Vietnam.

Despite all these changes the study of Marxist regimes remains in its infancy and continues to be hampered by constant and not always pertinent comparison with the Soviet Union, thus somewhat blurring the important underlying common theme—the 'scientific theory' of the laws of development of human society and human history. This doctrine is claimed by the leadership of these regimes to consist of the discovery of objective causal relationships; it is used to analyse the contradictions which arise between goals and actuality in the pursuit of a common destiny. Thus the political elites of these countries have been and continue to be influenced in both their ideology and their political practice by Marxism more than any other current of social thought and political practice.

The growth in the number and global significance, as well as the ideological political and economic impact, of Marxist regimes has presented scholars and students with an increasing challenge. In meeting this challenge, social scientists on both sides of the political divide have put forward a dazzling profusion of terms, models, programmes and varieties of interpretation. It is against the background of this profusion that the present comprehensive series on Marxist regimes is offered.

This collection of monographs is envisaged as a series of multi-disciplinary textbooks on the governments, politics, economics and society of these countries. Each of the monographs was prepared by a specialist on the country concerned. Thus, over fifty scholars from all over the world have contributed monographs which were based on first-hand knowledge. The geographical diversity of the authors, combined with the fact that as a group they represent many disciplines of social science, gives their individual analyses and the series as a whole an additional dimension.

Each of the scholars who contributed to this series was asked to analyse such topics as the political culture, the governmental structure, the ruling party, other mass organizations, party-state relations, the policy process, the economy, domestic and foreign relations together with any features peculiar to the country under discussion.

This series does not aim at assigning authenticity or authority to any single one of the political systems included in it. It shows that depending on a variety of historical, cultural, ethnic and political factors, the pursuit of goals derived from the tenets of Marxism has produced different political forms at different times and in different places. It also illustrates the rich diversity among these societies, where attempts to achieve a synthesis between goals derived from Marxism on the one hand, and national realities on the other, have often meant distinctive approaches and solutions to the problems of social, political and economic development.

University College   *Bogdan Szajkowski*
Cardiff

Contents

List of Illustrations and Tables

Map

Figure

Tables

Basic Data

Official name	Co-operative Republic of Guyana
Capital	Georgetown
Land area	214,970 sq. km.
Road network	2,915 km.
Population (1980)	758,000
Population density	3.7 per sq. km.
Urban population	314,000
Population growth	2.1 per 100 per annum
Ethnic groups (1980, %)	East Indians, 50.16; Africans, 30.00; Coloureds, 13.20; Amerindians, 4.60; Portuguese, 1.00; Chinese, 0.60; Europeans, 0.40
Official language:	English
Minority languages:	Hindi, Urdu, Amerindian dialects
Political structure	
Constitution	20 February 1980
Administrative divisions	10 Regions
Highest legislative body	National Assembly and President
Highest executive	President and Cabinet
President	Hugh Desmond Hoyte since August 1985
Prime Minister	Hamilton Green since August 1985
Ruling party	People's National Congress since 1964
Leader	Hugh Desmond Hoyte since August 1985
General Secretary	Ranji Chandisingh since 1984
Party membership (1983)	8,300 or about 1 per cent of population
Official opposition party	People's Progressive Party (Marxist/Leninist) since 1968
General Secretary	Cheddi Jagan
Economy	
Labour force (1982)	308,000
GNP at market prices (1983)	G$1,296m.
GNP per capita (1983)	G$1,563
Monetary unit	Guyana dollar; (1984) US$1.00 — G$4.30

State budget (1981)   Revenue   G$1,009.0m.;   Expenditure
                                 G$1,176.6m.

Main natural resources   Bauxite, timber, fishing, agriculture
Land tenure   Freehold and leasehold; no limit except on
                                 government schemes

Main crops   Rice and sugar
    Main exports (1982 % of total
exports)   Bauxite 39; Sugar 36; Rice 8
    Main imports (1982 % of total
imports)   Consumer goods, 13; Intermediate goods
                                 (including fuel and chemicals), 69.5; Capital
                                 goods, 16.5

    Destination of exports
(1983 % of total exports)   Britain, 30; US, 17; Caricom, 16
    Main trading partners   Britain;   US;   Caricom;   Canada
                                 Average annual growth 1970/80 1981/82
    Food production per capita % —1.1 —3.3
    Agriculture   1.2 —1.2
    GDP   1.3 —6.6
    Foreign debt   US$1.3bn.
    Foreign aid (1983)   USAID G$3.9m.; UN G$1.4m.; Canada
                                 G$0.6m.; Others G$6.0m.

Education and health
    Adult literacy   91%
    Primary 1979/80   424 schools; 6,021 staff; 164,830 students
    Secondary 1979/80   87 schools; 2,513 staff; 45,595 students
    Technical 1979/80   12 colleges; 242 staff; 3,595 students
    Teacher Training 1979/80   3 colleges; 106 staff; 1,052 students
    University 1979/80   1, University of Guyana opened October
                                 1962: 1,889 students

Life expectancy (1985)   70 years
Hospital beds per 100 of
population (1982):   4.3
Population per physician (1982): 10,165
Infant mortality (1982)   50.5 per 1,000

Defence expenditure as % of
total expenditure (1982):   7.6
Armed forces   Guyana Defence Force, regular army of
                                 7,000; People's Militia and paramilitary
                                 Guyana National Service of 5,000

Foreign relations:	Diplomatic and consular relations with countries, at least sixteen of which have representatives in Georgetown
Membership of international organizations:	UN, June 1966, 118th member; Commonwealth, May 1966, 23rd member; Caricom, 1973; Non-Aligned Movement, 1979; IMF and World Bank, September 1966; Africa, Caribbean and Pacific Group of Countries, July 1973; International Bauxite Association, March 1974; Inter-American Development Bank, November 1976; International Finance Corporation and International Development Association, January 1976; Latin America—New Economic System, October 1975.

Population Forecasting

The following data are projections produced by Poptran, University College Cardiff Population Centre, from United Nations Assessment Data published in 1982, and are reproduced here to provide some basis of comparison with other countries covered by the Marxist Regimes Series.

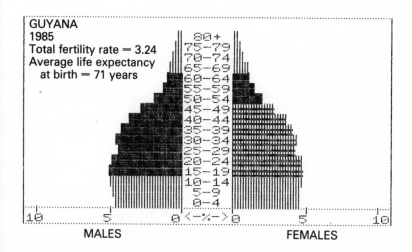

GUYANA
1985
Total fertility rate = 3.24
Average life expectancy at birth = 71 years

MALES   FEMALES

Projected Data for Guyana 1985

Total population ('000)	981
Males ('000)	491
Females ('000)	490
Total fertility rate	3.24
Life expectancy (male)	67.7 years
Life expectancy (female)	73.3 years
Crude birth rate	27.9
Crude death rate	5.2
Annual growth rate	2.27%
Under 15s	36.75%
Over 65s	4.05%
Women aged 15–49	25.75%
Doubling time	31 years
Population density	5 per sq. km.
Urban population	22.3%

Abbreviations

ALCAN	Aluminium Company of Canada
BGEIA	British Guiana East Indian Association
BGTUC	British Guiana Trades Union Council
Caricom	Caribbean Community and Common Market
CASWIG	Conference on the Affairs and Status of Women in Guyana
CCWU	Clerical and Commercial Workers' Union
CEC	Central Executive Committee of the People's National Congress
GIWU	Guiana Industrial Workers' Union
GAWU	Guyana Agricultural Workers' Union
GBSU	Guyana Bauxite Supervisors' Union
GDF	Guyana Defence Force
GMWU	Guyana Mine Workers' Union
GNS	Guyana National Service
GUYSTAC	Guyana State Corporation
ICFTU	International Confederation of Free Trade Unions
LCP	League of Coloured People
MP	Member of Parliament
MPCA	Manpower Citizens' Association
NAACIE	National Association of Agricultural, Commercial and Industrial Employees
NLF	National Labour Front
PAC	Political Affairs Committee
PNC	People's National Congress
PPP	People's Progressive Party
PSU	Public Service Union
TUC	Trades Union Congress
UPD	United Democratic Party
UF	United Force
UGSA	University of Guyana Staff Association
WFTU	World Federation of Trade Unions
WPA	Working People's Alliance
WPEO	Women's Political and Economic Organization
WPO	Women's Progressive Organization
WRSM	Women's Revolutionary Socialist Movement
YSM	Young Socialist Movement

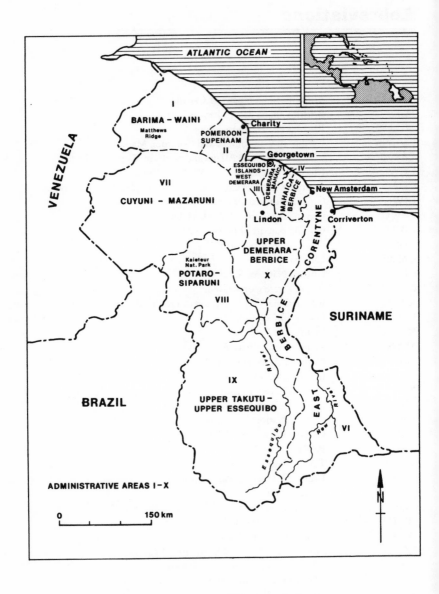

ADMINISTRATIVE AREAS I–X

0   150 km

Introduction

Forbes Burnham died of a heart attack on 6 August while undergoing a minor operation for a throat ailment. This manuscript was completed on that very day, so it falls to us to say a few words about the contributions Burnham made to Guyana during his twenty-one years in power. The media in Guyana are 90 per cent state-owned and very much under the direction of the ruling party so that, over the next few weeks, or perhaps months, the Guyanese people will be kept constantly 'informed' of Burnham's 'massive' contribution. On the other hand, his many detractors will construe his death as merely bringing to an end one epoch of a tyranny which he had set up and which is likely to continue until the people of Guyana are able to force the regime from office and to ensure that it accounts for its 'crimes'.

After the dust has settled, historians, more qualified than us, will take on the task of assessing the Burnham era and may, with hindsight, not be either as laudatory or as damning. Yet we believe that they will tend towards the latter. Any objective assessment of Burnham's achievements cannot simply highlight this or that successful programme initiated by him or instituted during this time. (On reflection, it may even be difficult to find many such successful programmes.) A correct assessment must be comparative: made against the background of comparable achievements in neighbouring and related countries and within the possibilities which independence had opened up. As the contents of this book will demonstrate, if this procedure is followed there will be little praise and much blame.

Burnham's personality, a mixture of intellectuality, ideological sophistication, suavity, and a degree of tolerance, has left an indelible imprint upon Guyanese society and particularly on those who knew him. He was an autocratic leader but the impression has been left that this resulted from a peculiar combination of socio-ideological factors. He seems to have held a particular conception of power which was very prevalent in the nineteenth and first half of the twentieth centuries. Democratic government was something which strong men succumbed to only if the rabble had become too powerful. Burnham did not hate the rabble: they just were rabble and had to be educated to his standards—hence his commitment to socialism and his perennial emphasis on the need for more and more schools.

We will argue throughout this book that from the ideological stand-point Burnham believed that fortune had placed him in a unique historical situation which would allow him to construct socialism, even radical socialism, on the American continent. Others reinforced this view at every opportunity and Burnham came to believe that it was his historic duty to protect that operational context even when it involved dictatorial politics which were in direct contradiction to his claim to be just what the rabble was not: educated and sensitive, not only to the best food and drink (which he loved and availed himself of at every opportunity), but to the human perspective.

However, after two decades of PNC rule it is still possible to marshal a credible case that the nation has made little progress and that there is little doubt that Guyana is the most politically repressive country in the Commonwealth Caribbean. One writer has claimed that a 'repressive escalator' is in force. For the most part, those who have taken over the reins of office are not known for their concern for human rights: quite the contrary. But leaders often use other men to take the blame while the leader himself can appear conciliatory, and perhaps that is very much a part of what has happened during the Burnham era. Guyanese will hope that with their accession to power the 'new men' will recognize, at least implicitly, that in the final analysis the power they hold belongs to the people, to be used for their benefit and not to the detriment of individuals under the varying pretexts of protecting the collective good.

This is a study of the political transformation which has taken place in Guyana. As the reader will see, the statements of relative under-development and repression are only broad conclusions which are evident from any study of the empirical data. However, although these conclusions need to be stated, this rather bald presentation conceals a complex assortment of objective conditions, motivations and percep-tions. Our attempt to put these into a sensible explanatory framework has been most rewarding, and we trust that it will contribute to a more realistic assessment of the Guyanese predicament.

This volume began life as the result of a short period spent by one of the authors teaching at the Co-operative College in Guyana where the co-author is Principal. What germinated at Kuru-kuru on the Linden highway has seen fruition in Cardiff and it is ample testimony to the Guyanese author's knowledge that the study has emerged at all, as in addition to writing the bulk of the text, he has patiently complemented the non-Guyanese author's view of socio-political relations in Guyana. It will be appreciated that this introduction is a joint effort, although it is the strongly-held view of one of the authors, non-Guyanese, made against forceful objections, that this provides the appropriate setting in which to accord an acknowledgement of gratitude for his Guyanese collaborator's considerable contribution.

Both authors wish to record their warm thanks to Bogdan Szajkowski, whose help and guidance and alternations between the carrot and the stick have, we are sure, gone far beyond the call of a series editor's duties. It is a salutary experience working in the same institution as such an energetic editor and, indeed, it is a sure guarantee of getting the work completed.

In addition, we are greatly indebted to Dr Cheddi Jagan, the respected Caribbean Marxist leader, who, despite the pressures involved in the preparations for his party's Congress, gave his valuable time to read the manuscript and make many constructive comments.

We also wish to thank Ralph Ramkaran, Clement Rohee and Feroze Mohamed for reading the manuscript and making valuable contributions. Finally, our gratitude to Josephine Whitehead, whose editorial patience and tolerance made the compilation of this document relatively simple. The analysis and sentiments are, of course, essentially our responsibilities.

Henry B. Jeffrey and Colin Baber
Cardiff
August 1985

1 The Geographical and Historical Setting

In colonial times schoolchildren were taught that Guiana was the only British colony on the mainland of South America, a simple geographic fact which disguised a complex social and political past. In 1493, in recognition of the voyages of discovery encouraged and financed by the rulers of Portugal and Spain, Pope Alexander VI divided the New World between these two principalities. However, this division was in conflict with the geopolitical ambitions of other European rulers and by the first quarter of the sixteenth century they began their attack upon the Iberian monopoly.

In 1581 the Netherlands renounced its allegiance to the Spanish Crown and set about establishing a colonial empire of which Guiana was to be a part. When the Dutch landed in Essequibo in that year they found that the other Europeans who had been living there had been driven off by the Indians. In fact, the Spaniards had been making attempts to settle the area since the 1530s.

Guiana also provides the setting for the romance of El Dorado. The conquest of the Aztecs and the Incas and the huge wealth which flowed into the Spanish kingdom dazzled the minds of the European ruling class and for a time El Dorado became a focus of their dreams. Sir Walter Raleigh made his last voyage to the area in 1617 and was only one of many who spent large fortunes and much time fitting out voyages to the imperial city of Manoa, said to be the capital of El Dorado. Raleigh claimed to have had intimate knowledge of its location and wealth and insisted that it '. . . hath more abundance of gold than any part of Peru and as many or even more great cities.' (Adamson and Holland, 1969, p. 232).

The Treaty of Munster (1648) granted independence to the Netherlands and allowed it to keep the colonial possessions it already held and those it would acquire in the future. Guiana fell into the former category for the Dutch West India Company, formed in 1621, had already taken control of lands in the Essequibo. In 1627 the colony of

Berbice came into being, when the company made a private grant of land to Abraham Van Peere and, although the West India Company considered the intermediate area of Demerara to be its property, it was not until 1745 that it was finally open to colonization. The three colonies of Essequibo, Demerara and Berbice are separated by three similarly named rivers, and form the three counties of present-day Guyana. There had been some administrative unity between Essequibo and Demerara, but it was in 1831, under British rule, that the three colonies were formally united.

Geographical setting

Guyana has a land area of 214,970 sq.km. On its north-western and south/south-western borders lie its huge neighbours, Venezuela and Brazil respectively, with Surinam as its easterly neighbour, bordering on the county of Berbice. The three major rivers, the Essequibo, Demerara and Berbice, flow into the Atlantic Ocean which is to the north and provides a coastline of some 432 kms.

Geographically, the country is divided into three main areas: a coastal plain, a forest zone and a savanna. Of the population of 758,000 people, 90 per cent live on the coastal plain which is alluvial mud and varies between 15 and 65 km. in width. At high tide the coastlands lie below sea level by as much as 1.5 m. in some parts. In fact, economic activity was only made possible at all through Dutch ingenuity in the construction of dams, dykes and canals and a huge expenditure of slave labour. However, notwithstanding the effort which still goes into the maintenance and development of this hydrographical system, drainage continues to be poor.

Generally, the geographical and agricultural zones correspond. The bulk of agricultural production takes place on the coast. The earliest settlers had grown cotton, tobacco and sugar but when, in the seventeenth and eighteenth centuries, sugar became one of the most profitable items of international trade, the Guiana colonies, like their West Indian neighbours, were specifically geared to its production. The planters did all they could to discourage the development of alternative economic activities which could have provided the labouring population with a degree of independence from the sugar plantations. Even the cultivation of rice was discouraged when it was discovered that the slaves were cultivating it as a staple, and it only became an important economic activity in the early decades of this century.

Geologically, the forest zone consists of an eroded plateau from which rise the Pakaraima Mountains and Kaieteurian plateau. It supports a significant timber industry and limited quantities of gold and diamonds are also mined. In April 1982 a Canadian company struck oil in the west of the Essequibo region, but after rising to 400 barrels per day, production fell to 40 and was abandoned. In 1983 an American company began exploration on the Atlantic coast and the Government plans to sink wells offshore in the Corentyne region, though no significant finds have so far been announced.

The savanna zone, and particularly the Rupununi valley which is to the extreme south-west of the country, is the centre of the cattle industry. Pasturage is of low quality and the industry has been declining in recent years. Immediately beyond a swampy barrier, which separates the coastal plain from the interior zone, about 100 km. up the Demerara and Berbice rivers, bauxite is mined.

Guyana has a subtropical climate, with two wet and two dry seasons annually. High temperature ranges are to be found in the hinterland but nowhere are they extreme. Average temperature is 27C (80F) and average rainfall is 1,520mm. (60 in.) per year inland, rising to between 2,030mm. (80 in.) and 2,540mm. (100 in.) on the coast. The capital, Georgetown, stands at the mouth of the Demerara river and has a population of about 180,000. The other major town is New Amsterdam, the most important town in Berbice, which stands at the mouth of the Berbice river. The country is south of the hurricane belt and so escapes the periodic devastations of the Caribbean storms.

Historical setting: a border controversy

Geographically, Guyana is on the South American mainland, but politically, economically and culturally it resembles the island states of the Commonwealth Caribbean. This is of course due to their similar colonial legacy: an initially turbulent history during which they rapidly changed hands according to the vicissitudes of European geopolitics, finally settling down to a lengthy period of British domination. For example, the War of American Independence began in 1775 and in 1778 France and its allies entered the war in support of the colonies. In 1780, the British captured the Dutch colonies in Guiana, but in 1783, on behalf of their Dutch ally, the French expelled the British and ruled the colonies until after the Treaty of Versailles when they were returned to the Dutch.

As a result of these manoeuvres, Guiana even savoured eighteenth-century republicanism. In 1795, the plantocracy refused to throw in its lot with William of Orange and his English supporters, as a result of which the Dutch governor left the colonies of Essequibo and Demerara, and a Republic was declared. However, the Republic did not survive very long for, in 1796, the colonies were once again surrendered to the British. In 1802 the Peace of Amiens returned the colonies to the Dutch, causing some consternation among the solid British settlements which had given wholehearted support to the British occupiers. But they worried unduly, for the British were back again the following year, by which time the Peace of Amiens lay in tatters. In April 1814 Napoleon fell and the fate of the colonies was sealed: the London Convention of that year ceded them to Britain.

These political disturbances provide the backcloth to one of the most intractable issues confronting the present Co-operative Republic: the Guyana/Venezuela border dispute. Guyana also has border trouble with Surinam, which claims 15,540 sq.km. of its territory in the New River area, but this dispute is between countries of almost similar size and the claim is small in relation to Venezuela's demand for 137,270 sq.km., or almost two-thirds, of Guyana.

The Convention of 1814 gave the Dutch colonies of Essequibo, Demerara and Berbice to the British but in the 1840s Venezuela laid its first formal claim to the whole of the Essequibo. It stated that the land in that area had belonged to Spain by right of discovery recognized by the Papacy and by right of settlement and that it had therefore passed to Venezuela. Great Britain was the stronger power at the time and refused to compromise until Venezuela acquired the support of the United States of America, which invoked the Monroe Doctrine, stating that the American continent is closed to further colonization. According to President Cleveland of the United States, Britain intended to increase its territory in contravention of that Doctrine. He therefore called upon Congress to organize a Boundary Commission to determine what land was due to Britain and stated his country's intention to enforce the Commission's recommendation. Before the Commission had completed its work Britain agreed to arbitration. The Treaty of Arbitration was signed in Washington on 2 February 1892 and the present Guyana–Venezuela border was fixed in 1899 by the tribunal which resulted from that Treaty. The new boundary was agreed upon and the documents were signed by the parties early in the new century.

Here the matter rested for sixty years, until August 1962, when Venezuela informed the United Nations that it could no longer abide by the decision of 1899. The reason given was that Mr Mallet-Prevost, a junior member of the team of lawyers which represented Venezuela at the tribunal, had left a memorandum among his papers in which he accused Russia and Britain, through their members on the tribunal and particularly through its Russian Chairman, of making a deal which, in his opinion, deprived Venezuela of extensive and important territory to which Britain had no legal right (Schoenrich, 1949). Mallet-Prevost left the memorandum to be published after his death and it forms the core of the Venezuelan position which repudiates a sixty-year-old agreement!

The Venezuelans have provided many statements from those who were involved in the dispute at the time in support of their case but the evidence appears only to support the fact that, in his determination to present a unanimous decision to the world, the Russian Chairman of the tribunal may have forced the judges on the tribunal to compromise (The Boundary Question, 1982). As one independent commentator argued, of the fifteen volumes of papers in the British Foreign Office and of all the documents in Leningrad, there is not a single indication that a deal was made (Child, 1950). The fact that so much could be made of a dead man's opinion sixty years after the issue had been officially closed seems so absurd that more adequate answers have been sought elsewhere. The most widely-held view amongst Guyanese with a knowledge of the problem is that Venezuela was encouraged by the United States State Department to raise the issue in 1962 when the latter was not having much success in its attempt to remove the Marxist orientated Government in Guyana. After all, the Venezuelans must have known of the Mallet-Prevost papers since the late 1940s and it does appear too much of a coincidence that the issue arose when it did.

Since 1962 many attempts have been made to find a solution to the problem. There have been tripartite examinations of the historical document, ministerial meetings and, in 1966, a Mixed Commission was set up to seek a satisfactory solution to the controversy concerning the validity of the 1899 award. The four-year term of the Commission expired without the dispute having been solved but on 6 June 1970 the Protocol of Port-of-Spain was signed which provided for a period of twelve years during which the parties were to seek a solution to the controversy and refrain from making territorial claims upon each other. The Protocol was to have been automatically renewed if neither party objected to its continuance, but in April 1981 Venezuela gave notice of its unwillingness to let the issue drag on. Other peaceful means are available to the parties, both of whom have disclaimed the use of violence. Upon Venezuela's decision not to continue the Protocol, Guyana stated its preference for a judicial solution, but it has agreed to Venezuela's suggestion that the Secretary-General of the United Nations be allowed to decide how the dispute should be settled.

Guyana has accused its larger neighbour of many acts of political and economic aggression. In September 1966, Guyana reported that Venezuelan troops had occupied its half of the island of Ankoko which is situated in one of the border rivers. Venezuela is said to have continuously blocked Guyana's entry into regional organizations such as the Organization of American States and is also said to have attempted subversion using the Amerindians who live in the border region. In 1981, Guyana's President, Forbes Burnham, accused Venezuela of economic subversion when it objected to a World Bank supported grant then being considered for the development of hydroelectric power in the disputed area.

Historical setting: the people

African slaves were taken to the Americas from the early decades of the sixteenth century and one of the first acts of the Dutch West India

Company was to secure slave labour for its settlers in Guyana. It must have been relatively successful, for in 1623 the colony of Essequibo is reported to have exported 28,000 lb of tobacco. While some slaves were initially taken from the local Amerindian population, most came from Africa and throughout its existence the Company sought to maintain a monopoly of this lucrative trade in people.

Labour shortages plagued the colonies in the early period and the Amerindians presented a tempting solution. However, generally speaking, the planters were unsuccessful in their attempts to enslave the Amerindians. They failed because, once captured, the Amerindians soon disappeared into the bush from where they had been taken. The Company eventually passed laws against Amerindian enslavement but these went unheeded by the planters who went so far as to encourage wars among the tribes in order that they might acquire children to be brought up in captivity. These activities, added to the new diseases introduced by the Europeans, decimated the Amerindian population, which has not yet recovered. In the 1660s, a conservative estimate placed their number at about 50,000 (Webber, 1931, p. 16); over three hundred years later, in 1980, it was estimated at about 40,000.

African slaves formed the bulk of the labouring population. In the 1660s, the slave population was estimated at 2,500. In 1812, five years after the abolition of the slave trade, the slave population numbered 100,000 and it is useful to note that in 1841, seven years after the abolition of slavery, the entire population, excluding the Amerindians, numbered 98,130 (Ibid., pp. 16, 133, 208). During the entire period of slavery, the labouring population fell steadily, requiring replenishment by new imports, so it is not surprising that when the slave trade ended in 1807, the population dwindled.

A major reason for the steady decrease in population was the brutal treatment meted out to the slaves, and after slavery, to the indentured labourers. Seven years was the average life span for a slave arriving in the West Indies. The conditions of slavery are already amply documented elsewhere, however, so we need not deal with them in detail here. Suffice it to remark that it has been said that it was impossible to think of a punishment or torture that was not inflicted upon slaves. In Guyana their treatment was so bad that in the early 1750s the Governor of Berbice proposed a 'Code Noir' to regulate how they should be punished. The mishandling of pregnant women resulted in a low birth-rate and a skewed sex distribution which, because of the nature of plantation work favoured the importation of men, did nothing to increase the size of the population. Many slaves also practised primitive but effective forms of contraception to avoid bringing children into bondage, and of course, the general state of medical and sanitary knowledge, particularly among the labouring masses, was also a contributory factor.

The slaves sought every opportunity to secure their freedom and more than half a dozen serious slave rebellions were recorded. One of the first took place in 1730, when, on a plantation on the Mazaruni river in the Essequibo four Europeans and five slaves were killed, and one slave was burnt to death over a very slow fire. February 1763 saw the beginnings of what was to become the most celebrated slave rebellion in the history of the country. The slaves on two plantations on the Canje river in Berbice rebelled, killing all those who stood in their way. Their ranks soon increased to about 3,000 as they took plantation after plantation. Planters, particularly those known for their cruelty, were mercilessly hacked to death. Under a leader called Cuffy, who is now the National Hero, the slaves held the colony for a year. It took support from neighbouring colonies and from Europe to defeat them. Approximately 50 per cent of the Europeans in the colony lost their lives, either in direct confrontation or as a result of the unhealthy conditions which the war created.

When slavery finally ended in 1838, the Negroes again attempted to free themselves from the clutches of the planters by purchasing abandoned plantations and settling down to village life. In 1842 the planters decided that adequate profits were only possible if wages were reduced. The labourers went on strike, from the beginning of January to the end of March when the planters capitulated. In attempts to force the labourers to submit the planters had evicted many of them from houses provided by the estates and had destroyed such subsistence crops as they had attempted to cultivate. Thus, at the end of what was perhaps the first strike in the colony's history, the ex-slaves were more determined than ever to acquire their own property.

Once it was realized that ex-slaves were interested in buying a plantation, the price rocketed. However, by the end of 1842, 15,000 acres of plantation had already been bought, for over a quarter of a million dollars. The plantocracy's belief that the Negroes had squandered the relatively good wages they had earned immediately after the abolition of slavery obviously had no foundation, so they continued to do all they could to frustrate the development of a free peasantry. The success of these villages would have forced the planters to pay yet higher wages and that had to be avoided. They flooded the villages, destroyed the fruit trees, levied heavy taxes, passed laws limiting collective purchase, etc. After slavery there was no labour shortage as such, only an un-willingness on the part of employers to pay a decent wage.

These villages, which still form the basis of local government in Guyana, were organized in a spirit of co-operation. A report in the London *Times* of 19 August, 1845, referred to their inhabitants as little bands of socialists. They were administered by management com-mittees democratically elected by their inhabitants: women had equal rights of participation. This was not entirely new in the colony: in 1812, Major-General Hugh Lyle Carmichael, an English Commander then in charge of the colonies, had abolished the Dutch constitution and put in its place one which gave political rights to women. Women lost these rights in 1849 and they were not restored again until 1928.

It is argued that the co-operative philosophy of the present ruling party is rooted in the aspirations of this village movement and the general tradition of mutual aid which formed part of the life situation of these early Guyanese and which, to some degree, has continued to the present day. However, the machinations of the plantocracy broke the resolve of these early villagers and their attempt at village construc-tion cannot be deemed an unqualified success.

With the end of slavery, a solution to the labour problem was sought in the encouragement of indentureship whereby immigrants were contracted to work on the plantations for a given period, usually about five years. Thereafter, if they so wished, they were to be returned to their country of origin. It goes without saying that much effort went into encouraging these immigrants to remain in the colony and, preferably, on the plantations. The planters had refused Chinese immigrants in 1811, but in 1834, partly with an eye to the racial imbal-ance, they introduced Germans and Portuguese. The experiment with the Germans was a disaster: at one point they even refused to go to the fields. In 1835, the first serious attempt at immigration was made when 429 Portuguese arrived from Madeira.

The plantocracy did not give up the attempt to import Europeans but it became obvious that adequate and sufficient labour could not be expected from that source and the search turned again to Africa and to India and China. In 1838 the first shipment of Indians arrived from Calcutta and 1853 saw the arrival of the first Chinese. By the time the indentured system ended in 1917, a total of 31,645 Portuguese, 238,979 Indians, 14,189 Chinese, 13,385 Africans and 42,343 West Indians had arrived in the colony (ibid., p. xvi). However, according to the 1921 Census, the country had a population, excluding Amerindians, of only 297,691 persons!

The conditions under which the indentured servants lived and laboured were little better than those which had existed under slavery. The conditions under which they travelled to the colony might have been marginally better than those which obtained under slavery but the death-rate was still appalling. Three ships left China for Guyana in 1852: on one ship 45 per cent of the passengers died and the other two had an average death-rate of 12 per cent. Out of the 811 Chinese who started the journey, only 647 arrived and there was not a single female among them. In fact, they were not to see a female of their race for another eight years.

When so many racial groups and cultures are thrown together under different and even conflicting conditions some degree of friction is unavoidable but the planters did nothing to mitigate these difficulties or to help to create a nation. On the contrary, they used these differences to divide and rule. Unable to enslave the Amerindians, they had used them to police and capture runaway slaves. Once slavery ended, Amerindians were of no further use and so were allowed to retire to the poverty of their forest retreats, totally neglected by the government. The new immigrants were used to keep wages down, thus creating immediate hostility between them and the Creole population. These early conditions helped to provide the backdrop to the racial problems which exploded in the immediate pre-independence period.

Historical setting: political developments

Initially, colonial political life was conducted by a small white ruling class of plantation owners and colonial administrators, but with the growth of multinationals in sugar and bauxite, the ruling group became more differentiated, though still of the same colour. From the earliest period the different roles which the administrative and industrial sections of this ruling class had to play provided them with somewhat different perspectives as to the nature and direction of colonial development and this was the basis of a fertile political setting. The struggle for dominance between these two sections of the ruling group stood at the centre of the constitutional quarrels of the period and an appreciation of it will help us to understand much of the constitutional developments which took place.

In about 1680 the Dutch West India Company promulgated what may have been the first constitution of the colony. The Commander of Essequibo was given complete administrative authority over the land and the people, but in the application of justice he was to be assisted by a council consisting of the Sergeant of the garrison and the captains of such ships then in port. In 1732 a constitution was promulgated for Berbice which contained the basis of government of the colonies for the next two hundred years. It established a Governor, a Council of Government and a Council of Justice. Members of the Council of Government were selected by the Governor from a list provided by the planters. Together, the Governor and this Council of Government comprised the Council of Criminal Justice, while a Council more representative of planter interests but chaired by the Governor made up the Council of Civil Justice. In the early 1740s, the College of Keisers, which was to be of great importance, was established on the Essequibo colony. Consisting of the officers of the Burgher Militia who were the Justices of the Peace and rural constables, it now formed the electoral college.

The so-called 'recall movement', whereby the planters made charges against the Governor and his administration and begged the colonial authority to remove him in the interest of colonial development, was an effective instrument in the struggle between the administrative and industrial elites. It was first used, and with success, against

Abraham Beekman in the 1680s. Another important weapon in the planters' armoury was the control they had over the imposition of taxes. For example, by 1784 the colony of Demerara had overtaken Essequibo as the centre of production and trade and it was decided by the Dutch West India Company that there should be a single Director-General in charge of both colonies with a subordinate Director for Essequibo. The new orders stated that the Court of Policy was to be nominated by the Director-General and not selected by him from a list provided by the planters. The plantocracy rightly saw this as an infringement of their right to have some say over the government which spent their money and so they refused to pay taxes. The Company was forced to appoint a committee to consider the issue and a 'Plan of Redress' was drawn up which remained the cornerstone of the colonial constitution up to the first quarter of this century.

The College of Keisers was increased to seven members, with Essequibo and Demerara having separate colleges. The Court of Policy was to be under the direction of the Director-General, with the Director of Essequibo sitting as an ordinary member. Each college provided a list from which the Director-General had to choose two members to sit in the Court of Policy. In 1812, Major-General Carmichael abolished the College of Keisers, having decided that it was treason for Dutchmen to make policy in a colony under British rule. The planters protested in vain and the College was not re-established until 1831, together with the British institutions of Chief Justice, puisne judges and petty debts courts. Trial by jury was not allowed since it was believed that the people were not yet ready for such an innovation.

Then, as now, the underlying theory of the state explained it as a universalizing institution, evolving a national interest from the particular competing interests of civil society. However, the colonial state had the added responsiblities of looking after the interests of a labouring class which was incapable of recognizing, much less articulating and defending, its interests. Therefore, although the administrative elite accepted the political and economic status quo, they were obliged to put up at least passive resistance to the more blatant exploitative proposals of the plantocracy if their position was to retain a semblance of credibility. As a result, the colonial state was much more successful in protecting the interests of the economic elite than those of the workers, even if the bureaucratic elite had its own interests to safeguard *vis-à-vis* the planters. Indeed, this conflict within the ruling class provided the first chink through which the forces of democratization gradually forced their way.

In 1837, the Mayor and City Council of Georgetown were elected for the first time. The property qualification of $3,200 was high enough to prevent some constituencies from having any voters. The Census of 1851 gave the population, excluding Amerindians, as 127,695, but the total electorate consisted of 916 persons. Politics was an activity reserved for the plantocracy and the administrative elite, but growing within the system was a middle group of non-white property owners and professionals who were beginning to make their presence felt. A section of this group began to articulate its interests through a Political Reform Club formed in 1887 and their aspirations provided the administrative elite with just the kind of rationale it needed to enhance its position *vis-à-vis* the plantocracy. Furthermore, sugar was no longer king: the planter lobby was not what it used to be and the plantations were increasingly falling into the hands of limited liability companies whose headquarters were in London, where they were easily influenced by the state elite in the Colonial Office. In the last decade of the nineteenth century, ostensibly to fulfil the aspirations of the native middle class, the state elite forced through a constitutional reform which did little in fact for this middle class but significantly increased its own power in relation to the plantocracy.

As the system developed, the Governor could in theory have passed any legislation without consulting the planters, but the Court of Policy, half of which was elected by the planters, acted as the executive. Moreover, the financial representatives were also elected by the planters and as a result they had significant influence over the finance and administration of the colony. The only reform they cared for was that which would reduce the Governor's power over legislation. The 1891 constitution abolished the College of Keisers and an increased electorate was now given the right to elect both the financial representatives and the Court of Policy, which was shorn of its administrative role. The Governor gained the right to select his own Executive Council but its function was advisory only. In 1911, the population, excluding Amerindians, was 296,041, and the electorate was 4,104. This meant that the non-white middle group had been allowed some limited access to the levers of power and it is not surprising that they considered the constitutional changes something of a victory.

The victory of the state elite had all the ingredients of a palace coup but since the changes were presented as the state's wish to fulfill its historic responsibility to the population it controlled, the new arrangements made a qualitative leap in the political process. Once it was explicitly granted (even if hedged by numerous qualifications as to education, employment and wealth) that the action had been taken so that the native people could begin to rule themselves, theory became practice and the colonial system was doomed. However, it was not altruism which led the state elite to formulate the position that it did. Representative theory, which the American War of Independence did a lot to entrench, demanded that those who controlled the state should only do so with the permission of the ruled. Although the colonial state could have pleaded special circumstances, once the Creole elite and then the working masses became politicized and began to demand their political rights, self-rule could only be delayed, not avoided. This process was in its formative stages in 1891: the ruling class was not broken; power merely shifted within it and the great mass of working people were no better off.

The Employers' and Servants' Ordinance of 1853 had made industrial relations a part of the criminal law and the Immigrants' Ordinance of 1891—the same year as the constitutional changes—did not reverse that situation. Indentured servants could be fined by the courts for almost any kind of misbehaviour. Indentured immigration did not cease until 1917 and of the 9,284 adults in indenturship in 1907, 2,019, or 20 per cent, were convicted under that law (Rodney, 1981, p. 41). The Immigrants' Ordinance had prescribed some rather liberal working hours, which the planters disregarded with impunity. The state justified its authoritarian stance on the grounds that it was necessary to protect a weak working class, but this was far from the reality.

There being no adequate means for working people to articulate and concretize their aspirations, in 1905 their frustration flowed into the streets. What began as a strike for increased wages ended in a riot in which 75 per cent of the inhabitants of Georgetown were reported to have behaved as if they had lost their minds. Seven people died in the fracas which developed racial and political overtones. The crowds were reported to have chanted 'kill every white man' and in this case their venom was aptly directed, as the whites were indeed the ruling group. Widespread strikes also took place on the sugar estates but at the end of the day the socio-economic conditions of the people were not significantly changed. However, from this time right up to independence in 1966, the working people made it their continuous quest to control their own lives and labour.

The wave of industrial conflicts which followed the 1905 disturbances led to Hubert Critchlow forming the British Guiana Labour Union in 1919. Critchlow is the undisputed father of trade unionism in Guyana and a pioneer of the labour movement in the Caribbean. Previous attempts had been made to form trade unions in Guyana but they were short-lived. Critchlow first came to public notice in 1906 when, at the age of 22, he was charged with assault during a labour dispute. By the time the British Guiana Trade Union Council was registered in 1941, there were fifteen registered trade unions in Guyana. The objective of the Trade Union Council was to protect and represent the national labour movement and it presented demands for widespread nationalization and the democratization of economic and political life.

The strikes and disturbances continued into the 1920s and the economic crisis through which the colony was then passing made the conditions of the masses even worse. Then, as always, when the economy was in trouble the workers were expected to understand that wage reductions were a necessary condition for economic stability, but when times were better and they demanded increasing returns for their labour they were informed that the division of profits was not their concern. In 1926 a British parliamentary commission under Roderick Roy Wilson reported on the economic condition of the colony. It is significant that although it found that the old planter group and its supporters were devoid of popular support, it recommended arrangements to secure its representation in the political process. The state elite was now to use a situation it had created, i.e., the political weakening of the plantocracy, to further enhance its position. The 1928 constitutional changes, which brought Guyana into line with the Crown Colony System then prevalent throughout the West Indies, placed the planters firmly under the tutelage of the state elite. The latter was given the authority to co-opt the former into the newly-created Legislative and Executive Councils.

The state elite was now firmly in control of the political machinery but it could not justify its rule if it was unable to maintain social stability, so, elected or not, it had to make concessions to the popular forces. While the parliamentary commission was busy making arrangements to reverse the wheels of political progress by giving power back to an unpopular conservative section of society, Critchlow and others were thinking of broadening the democratic base to further the isolation of that section. In 1929, in conjunction with the British Guiana East Indian Association (BGEIA), the British Guiana Labour Union made representation to the Colonial Secretary for universal adult suffrage.

The 1930s brought further political unrest throughout the British West Indies and, in August 1938, the Colonial Office appointed the Moyne Commission to investigate and make recommendations. The commissioners found the people living in such deplorable conditions that it was thought imprudent to publish their findings during the war. In relation to Guyana they made certain constitutional concessions and in 1943 there came a reduction in property qualifications for electors and members of the Legislative Council and an increase in elected members to give them a majority.

Elections were not held until 1947 but in 1943 Critchlow and Ayube Edun (the latter had founded the Manpower Citizen's Association (MPCA) in 1937)—both representatives of labour—were co-opted to the Legislative Council and a year later Critchlow was appointed to the Executive Council, the highest seat of government in the colony. The planters had lost their struggle with the state elite and now the entire ruling class was under threat from a combination of the Creole elite and the working people. New tactics had to be employed: it was no longer a question of preventing the popular forces from actually participating in or even controlling the political process. It was now a matter of containing the people's representatives within an acceptable political framework. A new era had begun, but would the new leaders understand and accept its limitations?

2 Formation and Historical Analysis of the Regime

For some considerable time the elites in the colonies had set their sights upon political independence and the metropolitan centres, such as colonial Britain and France, which emerged from the Second World War were not politically or economically strong enough to withstand their demands. The prolonged struggle of the Congress Party which ended in Indian independence in 1947 and the independence of Ghana ten years later struck colonialism a severe blow from which it never recovered. However, as we have argued, the recognition that popular forces would sooner rather than later take political control of the colonies did not imply automatic acceptance of fundamental changes in the socio-economic system. To be more precise: capitalism need not be affected by such changes. Britain herself provided confirmation that properly organized capital had nothing to fear from the introduction of the popular vote and in the British West Indies there was not much to worry about. A conservative Creole middle class had long established itself in parliament, business and the professions. While progressive in relation to the plantocracy and its supporters, this middle class accepted the *modus operandi* of the system and only had the limited ambition of fully partaking in it. Guyana proved the exception to this general rule because the political leadership of the independence movement did not fall to the established middle class but to a group of radical intellectuals, epitomized by Cheddi Jagan.

The formation of the People's Progressive Party

Jagan is a direct product of the plantation system with its inherent poverty and humiliation for those of his race and class. His father was an estate foreman at Port Mourant in the county of Berbice. He attended local secondary schools and then left for the United States where he studied dentistry and married Janet Rosenburg, his life-long political colleague, before returning to Guyana in 1943. He claimed that it was during his formative years in North America that he became familiar with, and recognized the need for, a socialist activism and that this was later reinforced by his reading of Karl Marx's *Das Kapital*.

In the early 1940s party politics was still at a rudimentary level in Guyana. Individuals, not parties, were the focus of the political system and the parties were quickly put together to support people over whom they had little control. The Afro–Guyanese middle class, centred on the League of Coloured People (LCP), sought to maintain the Afro/Coloured monopoly of the influential political/administrative positions which were open to the native non-white elite, while the BGEIA vied for what it considered a fair share of those positions.

Almost immediately upon their return to Guyana, Cheddi and Janet Jagan threw themselves into the political fray. In 1946, together with Jocelyn Hubbard and Ashton Chase, they formed the Political Affairs Committee (PAC), which published a radical bulletin to aid the establishment of a political party based upon scientific socialism. At the 1947 elections, at the age of 29, Cheddi Jagan won an East Coast Demerara constituency from an array of establishment figures. The Legislature was still elected on a restricted suffrage and was primarily a debating chamber; the Governor and his Executive Council controlled the Government.

However, Jagan used the occasion to launch numerous attacks on the power structure. For example, he demanded that higher taxes be levied upon the bauxite industry and when the Government objected to the development of co-operative societies, which he believed would have helped to improve the standard of living of the Amerindian population, he accused it of capitalist bias. Little did Jagan realize that with such arguments he was providing the ruling class with ammunition which they would later use against him. The alliance between politics and the labour movement, which is common throughout the region, was also established in Guyana. After years of working closely with the labour movement, in 1949 Jagan became the President of the Sawmill Workers' Union. In the same year another event of political significance took place when, upon the completion of legal studies in the United Kingdom, Linden Forbes Sampson Burnham returned to Guyana.

Burnham was the Leader of the People's National Congress (PNC) from its formation in 1957 and the political ruler of Guyana until his death in August 1985. Of lower middle-class Afro-Guyanese origin, his father was the headmaster of a primary school in the East Demerara village of Kitty, which is now a part of Georgetown. In England Burnham became President of the West Indian Students' Union and moved in left-wing circles. When, in 1950, the People's Progressive Party (PPP) was formed, Cheddi Jagan became its Leader, Forbes Burnham its Chairman and Janet Jagan became General Secretary.

The disturbances which preceded the Second World War and the continued political agitation which followed both regionally and in Guyana forced the British Government to look at the system of political representation. The Waddington Constitutional Commission was appointed in October 1951 '. . . to review the franchise, the composition of the Legislature and the Executive Councils, and any other related matters in the light of the economic and political development of the Colony and to make recommendations.' The Commission conceded universal adult suffrage and internal self-government but it reserved certain powers of veto for the Governor which empowered him to suspend the constitution if the need arose. It was considered one of the most advanced colonial constitutions of the day and in the election which took place in 1953, the PPP won eighteen of the twenty-four seats. However, less than four and a half months after the Government took office, the Governor used his reserve power to suspend the constitution, claiming that the country was under the threat of communist subversion.

Why was the PPP so rudely thrown out of office? A brief review of some of its activities during its short period in government may help to provide the answer. It used its legislative majority to lift a ban which had been placed upon radical West Indians entering the colony; it repealed the Undesirable Publications Ordinance which was designed to prevent 'communist' literature entering the colony; it amended the Rice Farmers (Security of Tenure) Ordinance to provide them with better drainage and irrigation and protected the rights of tenant farmers. It also passed a resolution in the legislature asking the President of the United States to exercise clemency in the case of the

Rosenburgs (no relation to Janet Jagan) who were found guilty and later executed for being communist spies. But probably its greatest crime was its intention to pass a law which would have made it compulsory for employers to recognize trade unions which had the support of the majority of workers. This would have resulted in the sugar companies having to recognize the Guiana Industrial Workers' Union (GIWU) whose President, Dr J. P. Latchmansingh, was a minister in the PPP Government. Given that party's consistent championing of the workers' cause and its often-stated socialist intention, national and international capitalist interests became alarmed.

On the same day that the Labour Relations Bill was introduced into the House, the GIWU called a strike for recognition which lasted for almost a month. A government which made use of its industrial arm to cripple the very political and economic fabric which, as some saw it, it was its duty to maintain, must indeed have struck a colonial administrator as something out of communist revolutionary theory. Furthermore, senior PPP members such as Jocelyn Hubbard were known to be Marxists, Jagan, by his own admission, wasted no opportunity to expound upon the need for class struggle (Jagan, 1966, p. 67) and senior members of the party even carried the portrait of Stalin during demonstrations. It is usual to condemn the colonial administration for so rudely frustrating the 'will of the people' and, given that such condemnations are necessary and useful in so far as they help to create the environment for further liberalization, this is understandable. However, given what we know of the underlying principles of the colonial state, the suspension of the constitution was not unexpected. Indeed, it is interesting to speculate whether, in the present geopolitical context of the continent, the PPP would not be treated similarly today.

The PPP was now out of office and the Governor, with the aid of some nominated officials, ran the country until after the election of 1957. The PPP was the first mass political party able to win the support of both the Indian and African working class and intellectuals and, when coupled to its socialist oritentation, it posed a formidable threat to capital which sought to and succeeded in destroying it. In 1955 the PPP split into Jagan and Burnham factions but the national movement held together until 1957 when other African leaders left the PPP, claiming that it was racially orientated. With that, the national movement divided along racial lines—the Indians following Jagan and the Africans supporting Burnham.

The suspension of the constitution could not continue indefinitely given the pace of the decolonization process and the internal ferment and so the period of the 'interim' government was used to attempt to foster more acceptable leadership and weaken Jagan's position. Previously unavailable finance was made available to the interim government which was unable to utilize all of it in the available time. Jagan's supporters in the rural areas were major beneficiaries of the regime's attempt to bribe them away from the PPP but the attempt had the reverse effect as people came to realize that it was the very existence of the PPP which made such bounty possible. Moreover, racism began to play a greater part in the political equation and it proved impervious to such economic bribes.

At the political level the major tactic was to divide and rule and Burnham was the focus of attention. Peter Simms has stated that Burnham may have been recruited with the aid of the British communist party to strengthen certain weaknesses which were thought to exist in the anti-colonial movement in Guyana (Simms, 1966, p. 82). According to Simms, it may have been put to Jagan that a national movement could only be strengthened if a Negro leader could be found who was able to break the hold the middle class Africans had over the mass of urban Negroes. Burnham was to provide the lever to prise these people away from the conservative leadership and he understood that he would be made the leader of the movement. When the PPP came into being in 1950, Burnham was made the Chairman but Jagan became Leader. It appears that in 1948, the year before Burnham returned to Guyana, the Jagans provided leadership for a disturbance which took place at Enmore on the East Coast of Demerara. That, together with their activities in the trade union movement and Cheddi's work in the legislature, made the Jagans national leaders, respected by both Indians and Africans, as a result of which Burnham became less important. This may help to explain the persistent leadership problems which plagued the new party. Ashton Chase was to have been the first Chairman of the party but he gave way to Burnham. In 1952 and again immediately after the election victory of 1953, Burnham manoeuvred to challenge Jagan for the leadership. International capital was well aware of dissension within the PPP and used it to destroy the party. It was widely publicized that it was the adventurists within the PPP, headed by the Jagans, who were responsible for the colony not making political progress. Britain was willing to grant political independence but would not leave a group of irresponsible communists in control of the state. However, there was a moderate faction within the PPP—identified by the Robertson Commission which enquired into the suspension of the constitution (Constitutional Commission, 1954)—headed by Burnham, with which the British was willing to work once it could rid the party of the communists.

Burnham took the plunge and after some very involved manoeuverings the PPP split. Personal, ideological and tactical factors explain Burnham's behaviour. The fact that Jagan might have cheated him of the leadership was a factor, but ideologically Burnham was more inclined to the socialist/nationalist ideological position of President Tito of Yugoslavia and Mao Tse-tung of China. In 1960, Eusi Kwayana, then a close political colleague, praised Burnham for his undogmatic ideological approach. He argued that: 'The fact that we called him Trotsky or Tito and such things in his absence is proof that he never took the [pro-Soviet] line' (Kwayana, 1960). Burnham considered many of the party's Marxist/Leninist leaders to be senseless adventurists who were more contemptible since they failed to realize that by proclaiming their adherence to Marxism in its most radical form and at the drop of a hat they were building obstacles in the path of the country's independence. He also considered that it was possible to maintain the national movement without Jagan and the few others who were already recognized by international capital as people into whose hands the state should not fall. After all, he was the most popular Negro leader and Dr Latchmansingh, on whose support he could depend, was a moderate with as much support among the Indian community as Jagan. Burnham did not expect or want the national movement to divide along racial lines but it did and Jagan won every election until 1964 when international capital rigged the system to give the PNC victory.

Burnham's strategy was unsuccessful for at least three reasons. Firstly, Jagan was more popular than Burnham had thought. Secondly, Jagan criticized the prominent 'ultra-leftists' of his faction who then left and he recruited a number of Indian businessmen and farmers to broaden the ideological base of his group. Thirdly, and most importantly, the PNC continues to argue that Jagan's success rested finally upon his willingness to use the appeal of race to undermine the Indian support which would have gone to Latchmansingh. The PPP sees this latter contention as illogical since it claimed at the time that the Indians were not the majority in the country, and the party—particularly its youth arm—had many African members. The African middle classes in the urban areas had long been acquainted with such methods but in elections from 1957 onwards *apan-jaat* (vote for your race) politics became the order of the day.

The Jagan era

The constitution under which the 1957 election was held was retrograde when compared with its predecessor. Both the legislative and executive authority of the elected members of Parliament was counterbalanced by nominated and official members. Furthermore, every effort was made to construct a system which would operate against the Jagan faction of the PPP. In the faction's stronghold in East Berbice one constituency had 32,000 voters compared with 45,000 for the three constituencies in the Burnhamite area of Georgetown. However, of the 14 seats contested at the election, the Jaganites won 9, leaving Burnham's faction with 3, the African middle class United Democratic Party (UDP) 1 (in New Amsterdam) and the National Labour Front (NLF), led by an establishment Indian and intended to undermine the PPP's support in the rural areas, 1 (in the north-west of the country).

Jagan was able to consolidate the vote of the rapidly growing Indian population which at the time made up about 45 per cent of the population. Time was on his side and Burnham and national and international capital were not amused. Out of sheer frustration, the British were beginning to see Jagan as the only leader capable of taking Guyana to independence, but the United States had no intention of allowing a communist regime in the hemisphere.

After its defeat, the Burnham faction of the PPP conceded the designation 'People's Progressive Party' to the Jaganites and united with the

Negro middle class UDP to become the People's National Congress. Like Jagan, Burnham was not really a product of the establishment middle class and his new partners were suspicious of his socialism. However, they were even more worried about the growing economic and political strength of the Indians and the 'communism' of the PPP. The United Force (UF), a right-wing party representing the interests of big business, the hierarchy of the Catholic church and—through the church—most of the Amerindians and Portuguese voters, also joined in the fight to defeat the PPP.

For the election of 1961 the country was again gerrymandered but this time into thirty-five constituencies. Burnham promised to support the independence demands of whichever party won the election. But once again Jagan won and, not surprisingly, Burnham changed his mind on the independence pledge. The PPP took 20 seats, the PNC 11 and the UF 4—2 in the PNC stronghold of Georgetown. This UF performance definitely indicated that Burnham was not the force he was thought to be in the urban areas. On the other hand, Jagan now appeared unassailable and independence could not be posponed much longer. But if the British were prepared to wash their hands of Guyana the United States was prepared to assume responsibility, much as it did for the French in Vietnam. As already noted, in 1962 the Guyana/ Venezuela border dispute which had been finalized sixty years before mysteriously reappeared and more American 'trade unionists' entered Guyana in the eighteen months following the 1961 election than had done in the eighteen years preceding it! It was now widely accepted that the CIA used the trade unions in Guyana to undermine the PPP (*The Sunday Times*, 16 April 1967). The Americans also informed the British that the opposition's demand for proportional representation was the only way to remove Jagan. Although the PPP had continuously taken the vast majority of seats with the highest single percentage of votes, it had always polled less than 45 per cent of the total votes. In 1961, for example, with almost double the number of seats gained by the PNC, the PPP only received 2 per cent more votes (43 to 41 per cent).

It was well-known that the British and their American ally sought any pretext to avoid granting independence to the PPP and so the opposition, aided by the CIA, began a campaign of destabilization through strikes and demonstrations. The major opposition parties mobilized their supporters against every aspect of the PPP's programme. Burnham led a massive demonstration of some 20,000 people outside the Legislature in protest against the Government's budget, which he claimed was anti-working class. The campaign of destabilization under way, it was then argued that the PPP was unable to maintain order because it represented the minority of Guyanese. Independence should only be given after new elections were held under a system of proportional representation which would provide a government more representative of the people and, therefore, able to rule. For its part, the PPP opposed proportional representation, and with its eye on the growing Indian vote, demanded that the voting age be reduced to eighteen. It may also have calculated that this latter demand provided it with something with which to bargain and if perchance a compromise had to be worked out and it had to concede proportional representation, the lower voting age might have provided just the edge it needed to retain power. Naturally, the opposition objected to all PPP demands and refused to compromise.

A constitutional conference was held in 1962 but it broke up because the parties could not agree. The destabilization continued and Jagan has stated that he came to realize that, given the formidable forces which were allied against him, it was impossible for him to rule (Jagan, 1966, pp. 297–80). This is the only sensible explanation for the decision he took at the 1963 constitutional conference. As in the previous year, the 1963 discussions reached deadlock and the PPP joined the PNC and UF and agreed to abide by whatever decision the Colonial Secretary, Duncan Sandys, made on the contentious issues. When Jagan, a self-confessed Marxist who had broken the American blockade and traded with Cuba during the high-water point of anti-communism in the region, placed his future in the conservative hands of Duncan Sandys, he did indeed appear to capitulate. Sandys gave the opposition all they demanded.

However, much of the force of the above explanation is lost when one considers the degree to which Jagan protested against the Sandys decision. The PPP used its influence over the Guiana Agricultural Workers' Union (GAWU), which had replaced the GIWU as the militant but as yet unrecognized union among the sugar workers, to call a strike. Its intention was to demonstrate, as the opposition had done, that any other government would be untenable. The strike would have shut down the industry and the opposition was determined that it should not succeed. The sugar estates decided to use scab labour, mainly Afro-Guyanese, to break the strike and a nationwide racial disturbance ensued. By the time it ended one hundred and seventy-six lives were added to those already lost in the offensive to remove the PPP from office.

This was all to no avail, however: the die had been cast. The 1964 election was held under a system adequately rigged to rid the ruling group of Jagan. Proportional representation gave the PNC 40.5 per cent of the votes and 22 seats, the PPP 46 per cent and 24 seats and the UF 11.4 per cent and 7 seats. Acceptable leadership was now found: a PNC/UF coalition took the reins of government and, for the time being, the Jagan era was over.

A historical analysis of the regime

The decision not to form a PNC/PPP coalition government came as a surprise to many PNC members—particularly the youth. After all, it was a contradictory ideological decision, since both the PPP and the PNC claimed to be socialist while the UF was an unashamedly capitalist party. Furthermore, forced by the circumstances of the situation, Jagan had offered a coalition in which the PNC would have had parity of ministers and had also stated that the premiership was negotiable. The Young Socialist Movement (YSM), the youth arm of the PNC, voiced their concern and Burnham is said to have told them that he intended to destroy the UF in the not too distant future; something, he confessed, he could not hope to accomplish with the PPP. The obvious question is why contemplate destroying the PPP at all? Instead, why not amalgamate with it to repair and strengthen the national movement? But even if there is any truth in this explanation of why the PNC formed a government with the UF, it is minimal. With the overthrow of Jagan the ideological issues were settled in favour of the UF and Burnham had no choice but to join with that party. He could not have joined with the PPP when the rationale for the split with the PPP, the loss of life and property and the aid the opposition received from international capital was to remove Jagan's influence from government.

The Coalition Government

The Coalition Government took office and, not surprisingly, calm was restored. It is most ironic that to this day the PNC claims this to be one of its major achievements, when the violence and disruption were primarily instigated by the opposition and its allies. The Coalition Government broke the trade relations which the PPP had established with Cuba: the PNC later explained that this was done to placate its supporters who were the victims of Cuban arms which were sent to the PPP. What is more to the point is that the Government had to fall in line with United States' regional policy, for which it was duly rewarded with generous Western aid and loans which had not been available to Jagan.

In 1967 Antigua, Barbados and Guyana were the original signatories to the document which established the Caribbean Free Trade Area, which in 1973 became the Caribbean Community (Caricom), consisting of the majority of Commonwealth Caribbean countries. Regional integration has remained a central part of the PNC's external policy and in 1966 Burnham stated two other important elements: non-alignment and support for the peoples of southern Africa. Pointing a finger at the communist world, he argued that it would be intolerable for Guyana to have beaten back one imperialism only to succumb to another (Burnham, 1970, p. 194). The British who had previously not thought much of Burnham began to see the development of true statesmanship.

The economic policy of the PNC/UF Government was not a great success (although, when compared with the present economic situation, the contrary would appear to be true). The first development plan (1966–72) was drawn up by Sir Arthur Lewis and was based upon the Puerto Rican model which attempted to create favourable conditions to attract investment capital. Neither geographically nor politically could Guyana have been compared to Puerto Rico; it did not have the necessary access to American markets and the range of investment opportunities which made Puerto Rico attractive to investors. The plan was abandoned halfway through, leaving a weak industrial sector, neglected agriculture, high unemployment and a substantial debt. (See chapter 8 for a more detailed discussion.)

Burnham argued that the coalition broke down because the PNC could not implement the radical changes Guyana needed in company with its conservative ally. This is a strange statement, for, as we have seen, UF conservatism was never in doubt; it even objected to the formality of Guyana breaking with the British Crown to become a republic. The truth is that Burnham wanted total power and recognized that another factor was in play which would force international capital to support his bid to acquire it.

Even with proportional representation, the Indian vote was growing fast enough to prove a real threat. Contrary to public posturing, Burnham and the representatives of international capital were well aware that he had made no impact upon the Indians' support for Jagan. If anything, the underhand way in which the coalition came to power and the decision to work with the right-wing UF may have lost the PNC some support. But that aside, the elections of 1957 and 1961 had taught the PNC and its backers not to trust the vicissitudes of racial politics. Burnham had also learnt from the British that once one adheres as closely as possible to legal formalities, electoral manipulation is quite acceptable. So, in preparation for the 1968 election, the PNC introduced the Representation of the People Bill which made it possible for Guyanese living overseas to vote.

The UF opposed the Bill in Parliament but some UF and PPP members crossed the floor and voted with the Government to pass the Bill. The procedures outlined in the Act are open to easy manipulation. For example, on overseas voting in August 1968, the Ministry of Home Affairs in Guyana stated that there were 43,000 Guyanese voters in Britain, but figures compiled by the British Home Office and the London Institute of Race Relations showed that there were no more than 23,000 Guyanese in Britain over 21 years of age, and only considered that 4,700 of the 11,750 said to be registered in the United States were genuine (Manley, 1979). Granada television made a documentary film which demonstrated widespread fraud in the compilation of the voting register in Britain. Proxy votes, which stood at 7,000 in 1964, rose to above 19,000 in 1968. Naturally, the PNC 'won' the majority of these votes. But these are academic issues. No one accepts the validity of elections since 1964 and Burnham has publicly made the issue into a joke. In an address to a group of Caribbean co-operators in 1976 he said that it is not a question of who votes and how but of who counts the votes. Those who counted the votes at the 1968 elections did the PNC proud. The party gained 55.8 per cent of the votes and 30 seats. The PPP was allocated 36.5 per cent of the vote and 19 seats, and the UF received 4 seats for the 7.4 per cent of the vote it was given. The PNC claimed that the people of Guyana had rewarded it for bringing peace, independence and good government. Burnham fulfilled his promise to the YSM: the United Force was, to all intents and purposes, destroyed.

The Co-operative Socialist Republic

In 1961 the PNC had committed itself to use co-operative societies as the instruments for building socialism in Guyana but during the period of the Coalition Government only minor efforts were made in that direction. The Puerto Rican model, then in vogue, had much more credibility than an ill-defined co-operative strategy but by 1970 the Lewis plan was obviously not delivering the goods. Expectations were dashed, leaving much disillusionment among the party's rank and file members, who, in the first place, were not in favour of the coalition.

Very little had changed; there were a few shifts of personnel but these mainly benefited the lower ranks of the Creole middle class. The old conservative elements which supported the colonial political and industrial elites were still as entrenched as ever. Independence had not fulfilled expectations and, since the break with the UF was explained in ideological terms, the radical policies which this unity was said to have prevented had to materialize. On the other hand, this had to be done without alarming national and international capital, which had not so long ago demonstrated their ability to remove an unsympathetic government, and the PNC's own middle-class supporters. Co-operatives seemed innocuous enough, particularly since it was possible to claim a lengthy heritage dating back to slavery. They also fitted in well with the argument of a section of the radical Black Power movement of the day which denounced Marxism/Leninism as irrelevant to the Third World and called upon the new Black leaders to adopt ideologies more relevant to their cultural context (Glasgow, 1970, p. 140). Furthermore, co-operatives seemed to bridge the ideological divide, since they exist in both the capitalist and communist worlds.

In 1970 Guyana was declared a Co-operative Republic in which it was said that the co-operative sector would become the dominant sector of the economy and that the spirit of co-operativism would percolate throughout society. The regime proceeded to organize many nominal co-operative institutions such as the Guyana National Co-operative Bank but in fact, rhetoric aside, no proper effort has ever been made to plan and develop the co-operative sector which remains relatively insignificant. The obvious discrepancy between theory and practice led to much ideological confusion which increased as the regime started to nationalize the local subsidiaries of the multi-nationals which operated in Guyana: were these industries to be co-operativized and, if so, how?

The Lewis plan in shreds, the PNC Government decided that the country's economic development had to depend upon its own resources. Import substitution and increased taxes, plus a larger share of the revenues the multinationals made to put together investment capital was important to this new approach. In 1970 the Government took control of foreign trade through the Export Trade Bureau. This had the political advantage of ruining the commercial section of the old middle class which tended to support the UF, but in its attempt to garner more of the multinationals' profits the regime was forced into a nationalization process and by the end of the decade it had taken over some thirty-two companies for which it promised to pay something in the region of $G800m.

The early 1970s were good for Guyana's economy, although the signs of declining production were evident. The prices of her main exports rose on the international market and in 1972 a new five-year development plan was unfolded in which the Government stated its intention to find 60 per cent of the planned investment. The plan was based upon the stated intention to adequately feed, clothe and house the people within the plan period. In 1974, in his now famous Declaration of Sophia, Burnham committed his party to a stronger socialist line and spoke of the need for it to become paramount over the Government. In 1976 this socialist trend reached its limit when

Burnham, whom international capital had placed in office, declared that: '... the People's National Congress is seeking to lay the foundation of a socialist society based upon Marxism/Leninism' (Burnham 1976). (See chapter 8 for further detail on this.)

In the field of international relations the early 1970s were also most fruitful. We have seen that the Protocol of Port of Spain, which placed the Guyana/Venezuela border issue in abeyance, was signed in 1970. In 1972, on the initiative of Dr Eric Williams, the Prime Minister of Trinidad and Tobago, Barbados, Guyana, Jamaica and Trinidad and Tobago, the four leading members of the Caribbean Free Trade Association, opened diplomatic relations with Cuba and in 1973 the Caribbean Community was created. Guyana also took a leading role in support of the peoples of southern Africa in their struggle against racism and in the Non-aligned Movement. Such was its success that in 1972 Georgetown was the venue for the Conference of Foreign Ministers of the Non-aligned Movement.

Under the PNC Guyanese society has become highly militarized. It is estimated that about 20,000 to 30,000 citizens have some connection with the military or one of the paramilitary organizations. With the help of the army the regime has 'won' every election since 1968. By mid-decade the PNC appeared invincible: the UF was destroyed; on the face of it the economy and international relations were doing well and the regime had taken a strong ideological stand. Such was the PNC's apparent strength that even the long-suffering PPP gave it critical support in 1975 and some of its top ideologues left and joined the PNC, claiming that: '... it is the PNC that is taking all the concrete initiatives in terms of social transformation, while the PPP is merely reacting petulantly and seeking in some cases to go one better in words.' (Chandisingh, 1976, p. 14.) The Working People's Alliance (WPA), founded in 1974 by a combination of left-wing groups, maintained a steady if somewhat muted opposition. However, the bubble was about to burst.

In 1976 commodity prices turned against Guyana's exports at the same time as inflation accelerated. A current account deficit which was G$31.9m. at the end of 1975 became G$350.8m. in 1976 (Bank of Guyana Report, 1979) as the country sank into an economic depression from which it has not recovered. There are shortages of almost every item (even those traditionally produced in Guyana) and the black market makes a mockery of Government's attempts to set targets. By 1978 the Government was at the doors of the International Monetary Fund, but after unsuccessfully attempting to get it to meet its targets, the Fund has refused to give further aid and the parties are still locked in negotiation.

In the 1974 Declaration of Sophia, Burnham had promised a new national constitution which was to set the nation firmly on its socialist path: that document came into force in 1980. The new constitution does, indeed, institutionalize certain basic socialist aspirations, such as the right to work and leisure, equality of women and the right of citizens to democratically control their lives, but Burnham also used the occasion to make himself an executive President. This has been the last 'radical' act of the regime. In 1981 Ronald Reagan came to power in the United States and his virulent anti-communism has forced the PNC to drop its Marxist/Leninist posture. In 1981 Venezuela refused to renew the Protocol of Port of Spain and in 1983 the chief ideologue of the party was sent to take up the post of Ambassador to Brazil. At least for the time being, the socialist experiment has ended.

The modus vivendi *of the PNC*

By this point the reader may have become aware of a unique historical equation which has allowed the PNC to implement certain aspects of a non-capitalist programme and adopt, if only in theory, a Marxist/Leninist posture without being destabilized as has happened to many others in the hemisphere. To understand why this has happened one must grasp the multi-dimensional nature of the following framework.

From the standpoint of the United States, the important relationships of the framework are the following:

1. The PPP is an avowed Moscow-orientated Marxist/Leninist political party, as is evident from its political programme (*For Socialism in Guyana*, 1982). Preventing its coming to power has top priority. Thus, Christopher Able, in reviewing the report of the British House of Commons Foreign Affairs Committee which considered the situation in Central America and the Caribbean, noted: 'The

Burnham regime escapes probing examination in this report ...
The question whether the UK and US governments condone the
behaviour of the Guyanese government for fear that any plausible
alternative would realign with Cuba and the Soviet Union is not
even raised.' (Able, 1983, p. 476).

2. Historical forces have combined to give the PPP a stable racial
allegiance which will most likely provide it with a majority in any
foreseeable elections. All the resources used to dismantle that
support have not been successful. For example, recently, one of its
spasmodic allies, quarrelling with the PPP's decision not to boycott
the 1980 election, commented: 'Did not the one [PNC] without
much success, say to the Africans, "The Indians are voting, you all
had better come out and vote?" And did not the other [PPP] ... say
to the Indians, *with more success*, "The Africans aren't voting, come
out and vote. The observers are here and we will get a fair count"?'
(*Argument for Unity*, 1983, p. 38). What we have here is an indication
of what is likely to happen, and what the outcome is likely to be, if
there were any chance of a fair election in Guyana.

3. The PNC is a necessary evil. The United States and its allies are not
necessarily in favour of it; they are simply against the PPP and
communism.

The political strategy and policies of the PNC indicate that the party's
leadership accepts its position as the geopolitical reality. The PNC is
not a client of the United States and its determination to manoeuvre
within the constraints created by international capital must not be
construed as acquiescence in American subversions in the region or an
unwillingness to struggle against them. But the intensity of its opposition will of course be constrained by the party's determination not to
jeopardize its unique historical context. Three additional relationships,
more or less implicit in those above, need to be stated.

1. The PNC considers itself to be a socialist party which has been
accidentally provided with a unique historical context which, if
properly utilized, will allow it to gradually build a socialist society
on the American continent. For this reason the PPP, or some other
more radical Marxist group, must always be posited as its logical
successor and all steps must be taken to prevent the growth of a

significant right-wing party. International capital must have no alternative but to support the PNC.

2. The PNC also realizes that neither organizationally nor ideologically must it become indistinguishable from the PPP. The United States must be given the opportunity to choose between the policies of the PNC and those of the more radical group. Much of what the PNC does can only be adequately understood if one grasps this relationship. Co-operative socialism had none of the radical ring of Marxist/Leninism in the early 1960s and although it has recently been allied to that doctrine it still tends towards China and Yugoslavia rather than the Soviet Union. It is a Marxism which, to the chagrin of the PPP, continues to link the Soviet Union with imperialism and superpower status. Nationalized industries were paid for, some say too handsomely (Kwayana, 1976). Cuba and Chile had demonstrated the communist alternative and perhaps also the consequences. There are numerous political and formal economic ties with the communist world but in 1981 Guyana still exported 66.2 per cent and imported 52 per cent of its goods respectively to and from the West. The Caribbean Community accounted for another 17 per cent and 35 per cent respectively (*Bank of Guyana Report*, 1981).

3. But quite apart from geopolitical considerations, the PNC believes that if the PPP were to regain control of government its opportunistic racial posture would dictate that it tailored its policies to maintain a stable racial majority. This could lead to untold suffering for the other racial groups. Indeed, the PNC considers that since it is a minority party it is forced to make the kind of concessions to the other races which the PPP would not be compelled to make. In any case that party believes that democracy means more than majority voting and that the kind of fixed racial majority the PPP may have attached to it could hardly be termed democratic.

The above historical context is unique on the continent and is largely responsible for the difficulty that exists in categorizing the PNC. It has been called everything from a dictatorship to a genuine workers' government. However, what appears certain to us is that the leadership of the PNC is socialist orientated. The party's perpetual flirting with left-wing policies cannot be adequately explained in any other way. It is true that no significant organized conservative opposition exists in Guyana, but this is largely due to the PNC's policy and its leftist tendency cannot be explained by the need to placate radicals. When it suits the PNC these radicals are treated with the utmost contempt. A most recent demonstration of this is the Government's introduction of the Labour (Amendment) Act 1984 (which the Marxist PPP called 'one of the crudest anti-working class measures in a Western democracy' (GIB, March 1984, p. 1)) without as much as consulting the Trades Union Congress (TUC) where the radical left is well represented.

3 Guyanese Social Structure— Race and Class

Guyanese society has developed in a fashion which makes racial con-flict almost inevitable and post-war political and ideological trends have projected class as an important issue of political debate. Thus, while admitting that racial issues are important in Guyanese politics, the leader of the PPP claimed that what is normally forgotten when such statements are made is that Indians and Africans do not form homogeneous racial groups and that in the colonial era many middle-class Indian and African leaders served the interests of the white ruling group (Jagan and Karan, 1974, p. 4). Similarly, in seeking to debunk the demands that the PNC and PPP should unite, Burnham argued that unity of the parties could well lead to disunity among their grass-roots supporters as each party seeks to enhance the loyalty of its constituents by granting it more and more privileges. Furthermore, since many of the conceptualizations surrounding the demand for unity are based upon considerations of race and not of class, he enquired of his audience, 'Where is the socialist content to such a "unity"?' (Burnham, 1977, p. 12). However, all parties agree that social integration is impor-tant to nation building and that in Guyana race has been a divisive issue while class has remained largely subsumed. In this chapter we will trace the historical connection between race and class and consider some of the arguments which attempt to elucidate their functioning.

Race, class and slavery

In West Indian slave societies class and race were essentially un-differentiated. The ruling class was presented as the superior race and its culture was upheld as the superior culture to which all should aspire. This was possible because a combination of white European planters and a bureaucratic colonial elite who were for the most part both racially and culturally homogeneous constituted the ruling class.

Within this ruling group there were less important sections, such as the plantation managers who were employed to take on the day-to-day task of managing the estates and a few poor whites, a legacy of the criminal elements transported to work on the plantations and of the attempts at European immigration. Though by no means easy, social mobility was possible between these strata. Bad management, adverse weather conditions and world market conditions left some planters bankrupt while a few managers married into the planter class or were able to purchase plantations.

In Marxist terminology, the ruling ideology was that of the ruling class/race and the acquisition of European-ness became important for social mobility. The non-white peoples could not hope to reach further than the fringes of the ruling group for they lacked that important criterion of membership. They were the exploited mass, but the racial ethos created social differences even at their level. Unable to enslave or discipline the Amerindians for plantation work, the planters used them to police the slaves. Once slavery was abolished, the Amerindians were of no further use and were allowed to retire to live in benign neglect in their interior settlements.

The Coloureds formed an intermediate group of freemen, it being not unusual for a white father to set his concubines and children free. They were an important buffer between the mass of slaves and the ruling group but their legal and psychological situation was most precarious. They were allowed certain privileges, such as access to a degree of education which led to lower clercial occupations, and many more of them migrated to the urban areas where they became skilled workers, petty traders, dockers, etc. The psychological dilemma resulted from the demands of the ruling ideology which dictated that European-ness was the hallmark of success. The Coloured person could do nothing about his African ancestry but he was able to demonstrate through the conscious adoption of European values that he had left behind the cutural attributes of the slave and the 'nigger yard' and had acquired those of free men, i.e. of the Europeans. Throughout the colonies these free Coloureds were well aware of their subordinate status *vis-à-vis* the Europeans but sought to enhance their position in relation to the slaves. In 1817 a group of freemen in Barbados thanked the local legislature for granting them the right of testimony. That right, they said 'was all we wished for, having . . . obtained that we are perfectly satisfied and contented, . . . where slaves exist, there must necessarily be a distinction between the white and free coloured inhabitants, and . . . there are privileges which the latter do not expect to enjoy.' (Delson, 1981, pp. 85–6). When slavery was abolished and the process of decolonization began, the greater aculturization of these people to European norms and values placed many of them in the fore-front of the national liberation struggle.

At the bottom of slave society were the black slaves, of whom those who toiled in the fields were on the lowest rungs of the social scale. Field slaves were the most brutalized. Better treatment went to those slaves who were skilled, were domestic servants and/or lived in urban areas. The skilled slave was not only very useful to the plantation but was frequently hired out by his owner and this gave him a degree of status. The domestic slaves and those who lived in the urban areas were, if nothing else, not compelled to perform the backbreaking tasks of the plantation under the broiling Caribbean sun. It is significant that the two largest slave revolts in Guyanese history were led by 'house' slaves, which seems to bear out the contention that it was those slaves who had the opportunity and time to contemplate the better existence available to free men who were most likely to become discontented.

Race, class and the colonial system

The end of slavery could not and did not destroy the solidity of the ruling ideology because it did not significantly affect the hegemony of the ruling class. The existence of indentured labourers complicated but in no way radically altered the general position. European-ness was still the hallmark of what was good and the Portuguese, Chinese, and East Indians, who were brought in the so-called immigrant ships, at first accommodated themselves within that system and later came to accept it. By the end of the colonial period, just as the Coloureds and Africans sought social mobility by consciously throwing off the culture of the 'nigger yard', the socially mobile Indians were decrying 'coolie' culture.

The planters continued their deliberate efforts to divide and rule but it was now the Coloureds who were to see privileges, such as easy credit, which were not open to them, made available to the Portuguese and the Chinese who were pushing them out of the commercial sector. However, gradually the Portuguese, Chinese and a few Indians were developing into substantial businessmen and, together with the Coloureds and Africans who had established themselves in the lower reaches of the public bureaucracy, in teaching, the legal and medical professions, they became an indigenous middle class but one within which skin colour was still an important factor of differentiation.

It must not be assumed that once they acquired the requisite degree of education the non-white people had easy access to high-status jobs. Harold Lutchman wrote:

The fact was that although many non-white Guyanese qualified for admission to the public service, they were unsuccessful in their attempt to join what was generally treated as a select and privileged group, because considerations of race, colour, and family connections were important, regardless of academic qualifications which some persons possessed. [Lutchman, 1973, pp. 225–51]

The white group latched on to the top managerial positions in all the multinational companies. As late as 1965, in the large establishments which employed more than 400 persons, expatriates held 46 directorships and similar positions while Guyanese held only 6. Of the other senior management and executive positions, Guyanese held 94, while expatriates held 126 (Graham and Gordon, 1977, p. 13). Since the state and the large companies were the major employers of scientific and technical graduates and most of these positions were closed to Guyanese, those who studied abroad only returned to Guyana if they held qualifications which allowed them to operate as independent professionals and this partly explains why there is still a surfeit of Guyanese who enter the law.

This non-white middle class was radically nationalist, for nationalism promised material and psychological benefits in so far as it would open employment opportunities hitherto closed to them and would release them from the ideological dominance of a mainly European ruling group. That this middle class was nationalist rather than socialist is demonstrated by its voting pattern in the 1953 election. The radical PPP only received 25 per cent of the votes of high-status Africans, 46 per cent of the votes of the African middle group and 80 per cent of the votes of those in the lowest-status group. For the other races, excluding Indians, the figures were 27 per cent, 51 per cent and 66 per cent, and for the Indians, even though Jagan, one of the most popular of the Indian politicians at the time, was the leader, the figures were 52 per cent, 77 per cent and 92 per cent respectively (Green, 1974, p. 39).

At the bottom of this pyramid were the rural and urban Indian and African workers. In so far as there was a proletariat it consisted of both the urban workers, such as the dockers, and the factory and field employees on the plantations, but there was much overlapping, particularly in the rural areas, between this group and the peasantry. Many of the plantation workers had small farms which helped to supplement their meagre wages while many who would have considered themselves full-time farmers were occasionally employed on the estates. This was especially true at reaping time when there was a greater demand for labour and long hours and sustained effort did result in reasonable pay. But the racial element of class affiliation must not be forgotten. In dealing with classes in the Guyanese society of the day it would not be sufficient only to consider the individual's relationship to the means of production. The girls who worked as shop assistants in the large department stores in the capital were paid very little and, by the latter criterion, should be included in the urban working class, but since their employ came mainly through family connections and the light-skinned middle class held the area as their preserve, such a classification would say nothing of the actual living conditions or perceptions of these people.

The plantation system affected the urban and rural proletarians and peasantry much more fundamentally than it did the middle class. They were the first to suffer when the price of sugar plummeted and the last to be considered in times of prosperity. Particularly on the plantations it was not unusual for wives and children to be sexually exploited and abused by the plantocracy. As a result, this section of the population sought the total destruction of the plantation system, with its special schools, playgrounds, swimming pools, etc. They were much more radical than the middle class who wanted a transference of power into its care rather than any radical democratization.

Sociological explanations of race and class

Attempts have been made to provide some explanation for the racial violence which erupted out of this complex social fabric in the 1950s and 1960s but they suffer from many shortcomings, some of which we will consider briefly. The pluralist society model associated with M. G. Smith and J. S. Furnivall was one of the first to be applied (M. G. Smith, 1974; Furnivall, 1939). Very briefly, this model states that given fundamental cultural disjunctures in a society one section must monopolize power if the society is to be maintained in its current form. Smith paid little attention to class, analysing society primarily in terms of the existence of cultural segments with their own life-style which only have limited contacts in the market-place. Political interaction between the sections is marked by dominance, subordination or conflict.

Applied to colonial Guyanese society, the pluralist model or 'extreme type' (McKenzie, 1967) conceives of a society made up of Indian, Negro, and European subcultures (which are so different as to have become almost separate sub-systems) held together by the European monopoly of power. The pluralist model is not synonymous with a racial view of society for it is obvious that deep-rooted cultural differences can exist within the same racial group. The racial violence in Guyana could be explained by the breakdown of the European monopoly of power and the struggle between the two strongest sub-systems for domination which should eventually result in a new power relation. Therefore, the PNC's monopoly of power can be seen as instituting a new situation in which African/Coloured domination has taken over from the European. Of course, once racial/cultural differences remain highly differentiated one may expect an outbreak of violence to follow any weakening of the present power structure.

A problem with the pluralist position is that it does not tell us under what conditions violence becomes a necessary consequence of competition between cultural sections. It is obviously not sufficient to point to sets of logically incompatible values and say that conflict would occur between adherents of these values if one group was not dominant. Before violence breaks out it must be possible to provide proof that the society is held together by violence. In his arguments against pluralism, R. T. Smith is said to have held to a 'reticulated' model of social change (Depres, 1967). He doubted that the wide cultural differences which form the foundation of the pluralist position could have been empirically located in Guyana. He recognized the differences of race and culture did exist and could not be expected to disappear overnight but argued that social integration could develop upon the variety of religious and cultural traditions (R. T. Smith, 1961).

Pluralists such as Leo Kuper and Pierre L. van den Berghe (Smooha, 1975; van den Berghe, 1974) have moved away from the classical pluralist model of M. G. Smith and Furnivall and have added the dimension of class to pluralist thinking. Van den Berghe insisted that class and ethnic groups are analytically distinct and cannot be reduced to each other. This is a useful concession but the pluralist approach does not provide an adequate schema for analysing the internal workings of ethnic groups and inter-group relationships. 'It is not enough to say that ethnic groups and classes are fluid and permeable. One must also have a method of analysing the fluidity and permeability' (Brass, 1985, p. 16). The pluralists seem to demand only that we classify the institutions of the various ethnic groups, assess the degree of their incompatibility and possible line of conflict. The task of social scientists seems not to be concerned with the overall process of change. Thus, according to Leo Depres, these models are deficient for they have not adequately considered the dimension of action and organization which is important for our understanding of social change (Depres, 1967).

Moves have also been made to make ethnic group consciousness more prominent in Marxist analysis. Some so-called neo-Marxists have attempted to move away from the classical Marxist position which viewed class consciousness as the only objective form of consciousness and classified ethnic group consciousness as a form of false consciousness. In the statements by the leader of the PPP and Burnham given at the beginning of this chapter we find an objectified representation of class as the primary reality. The questions which have to be answered if political theorists, activists and policy-makers are to respectively explain, mobilize and implement policies for the eradication of this false consciousness must first give it objective existence, but for the classical and the modern Marxist such false consciousness is only allowed a temporary existence. Thus, although like the modern pluralists, the neo-Marxists recognize the analytical distinctiveness of class, ethnic and status groups and argue for the fluidity of their boundaries, even for them only class consciousness has an objective reality. Their concession is partial and internal to the Marxist framework. For example, Immanuel Wallerstein believes that the existence of the capitalist world and the class struggle within it is the objective reality and that status groups are 'blurred collective representation of classes'. The class struggle takes different forms in different conditions and ethnic group consciousness is only a distorted form of it in given conditions (Wallerstein, 1979).

In this analysis we have made no assumptions as to the permanence of ethnic group consciousness. Such assumptions are of little comfort to societies like Guyana where there has been large-scale conflict which no one can guarantee will not recur. If it is not permanent, ethnic group consciousness is most persistent and our 'starting point is to raise the issues of the conditions for identity formation among different groups in the society and to ask what are the consequences for group formation of different types of state strategies and policies' (Brass, 1985, p. 24). We have given consideration to certain aspects of the origin of group consciousness, the position and strategies of certain key groups and sub-groups, particularly those which controlled the state and various alliance strategies. For example, in the preceding discussions we have attempted to indicate how ethnic group consciousness was developed in colonial Guyana and how the white ruling group through its policy of divide and rule did little to help the process of nation building. However, one of the major obstacles towards national integration has been the physical separation of the racial groups and particularly the two major ones.

Cultural differentiation and family life

The pluralist argument that cultural sections existed in Guyana is true: they were particularly encouraged by the physical separation of the different racial groups. However, in recent times the process of modernization has led to a mitigation of cultural differences. One of the central factors in this process has been the persistence of a European value system as the dominant cultural form long after Europeans have been physically removed from the levers of power. One important area of institutional divergence which has been affected by the process of modernization has been the perception of family life held by the two major racial groups.

In 1980 the population of Guyana was placed at about 758,000, with 314,000 people living in the urban areas. Indians constituted 50.16 per cent of the population, Africans 30 per cent, Coloureds 13.2 per cent, Amerindians 4.6 per cent, Portuguese 1.0 per cent, Chinese 0.6 per cent and Europeans 0.4 per cent. Although the racial violence of the immediate pre-independence period reinforced the pattern of separation as Indians and Africans moved to racially safe areas, Indians, Portuguese and Coloureds are still to be found in African villages and vice versa. Only Indians and Africans formed villages in which they were the majority and approximately 45 per cent of Africans and Coloureds live in the urban areas where they form about 70 per cent of the population. Indians form just about a quarter of the urban population while two-thirds of the Europeans, Chinese and Portuguese reside in the cities. The Africans and Amerindians are mainly Christians while 84 per cent of the Indians are Hindus and most of the remainder Muslims (Kurian, 1982). This religious difference has been important in helping to create and maintain the various groups as distinctive entities with specific values and interests.

African family life could not escape the ravages of the plantation system. Most of the slaves were taken to Guyana from areas in West Africa with a tradition of polygamy and the extended family. But by its very nature there was no place for stable family life in slave society where the individual was a property to be sold at the whim of the owner. It is well-known that to avoid creating emotional bonds many females practised primitive forms of contraception to avoid bringing children into a world in which they had no control over them and where they would have been subjected to the vilest brutalities. Short-term sexual and emotional relationships and the promiscuity which took place between the white owner and many female slaves, formed no basis for the development of deep-rooted family responsibilities. Of course many female slaves found a relationship with their owners to be useful for it meant that certain privileges might be forthcoming and there was also the possibility of manumission.

Not only was family life precarious for the slave population but there was also an implicit recognition of the hypocrisy which lay at the base of the Christian system of monogamy. It was evident from the large number of Coloureds in the population that the much-vaunted mutual fidelity of Christian family life was not to be taken too seriously; marriage and the family appeared to have the moral force of a tradition and did not prevent extra-marital relationships. Thus, what one sociologist called 'value stretch' occurred (Rodran, 1966). The Guyanese African accepts what appear to be conflicting systems of values. He sees the monogamous Christian family as the ideal but in reality accepts many forms of informal union.

Bearing children or living out of wedlock are not stigmatized among Guyanese Africans although the middle class have always frowned upon it. Marriage was an important demonstration that one had moved away from the 'nigger yards'. As in most societies, the adaptation of middle-class values seems to follow closely upon social development, so the tendency in recent years has been towards doing the 'right thing' by getting married and avoiding the birth of illegitimate children. This process has been assisted by the Women's Movement which has orientated young women of all ethnic groups towards education and aspirations for independent careers. The increasing availability and use of contraceptives have also helped to prevent unwanted children. But perhaps the most important factor in this new orientation has been the unwillingness of the younger generation of women to be sexually exploited to fulfill the macho image of men for whom the conception of many children by different women enhanced their masculinity.

Although the tendency alluded to above is in ascendance many young women still became pregnent despite the strenuous efforts of their parents to shelter them from the opposite sex. The young woman is then usually condemned by her parents and, though less often these days, may be compelled to leave home. If she is forced to leave she turns for help to her other relatives or, less often, to those of the man by whom she has been made pregnant. However, either before or immediately after the birth of the child, she is usually forgiven and allowed to return to her parents' home. The girl may continue her relationship with the father of her first child, setting up house with him and eventually getting married to him some years later. Alternatively, they may split up, with both parties forming other relationships and eventually getting married in their thirties or even forties.

The woman will normally continue to live in her parents' home until the couple decide to set up house together but in many instances a split in the relationship occurs when the man leaves the area in search of employment. The children are usually left with the woman and if she decides to set up house or get married to another man they may move with her or stay with their grandparents. Therefore, at any given period, the African community is made up of a variety of households ranging from the nuclear monogamous family consisting of a couple and their children to a kind of extended family which includes grandparents, their children, grandchildren and other relations (R. T. Smith, 1956).

Unlike the Afro-Guyanese communities in which the nuclear family constitutes the ideal, in the Indo-Guyanese village the position is somewhat different. It would seem that a different kind of extended family is the traditional ideal but that the European nuclear pattern has become the norm. Upon marriage, the son is expected to take his bride and live for some time in his parents' home. This pattern is maintained largely because in the Indian subculture it is the duty of the parents not only to raise their children but to guide them through the early days of their marriage, which is seen as a step which each individual should take. Furthermore, part of the condition of marriage is that daughters should be provided with an appopriate dowry and, where necessary, it is the duty of the eldest son to help his father provide that dowry. By the sixth or seventh year, the son will have set up his own household with his wife and children but even before this his wife will have taken over the responsibility of looking after her own family, even to the extent of doing her own cooking. The system in Guyana rarely develops into a fully-fledged extended family in which a number of nuclear families operate as a single economic unit (Smith and Jayawardena, 1959).

Unlike the Africans, the Indians who were taken to Guyana may in fact have chosen their destiny but they did so under the pressure of abject poverty and in almost total ignorance of their destination. The plantation system has had a lasting effect on their family patterns.

Firstly, the recruiting agents were not concerned with maintaining families; their main concern was to acquire able-bodied labour for the plantations. As we have already seen, the number of women they brought to the colony was most deficient and, particularly in the early periods, this led to instability in the family. The caste system was more or less destroyed, with people uncertain as to which group or sub-group they belonged to and some even fraudulently claiming higher caste status. In India it was normal to marry within one's caste and sub-group or *gotra*, but the latter has almost disappeared in Guyana and few fathers of high status would pass up an opportunity for their child to marry into a wealthy established family because of considerations of caste. Furthermore, unlike in African villages, most couples in Indian villages are said to be married. Marriages may range from the legally registered ceremony to the reading of a few words in the couple's home by an authorized priest. No such latitude exists in the African context where the ceremony must be performed according to Christian writ.

The Western family pattern is also in the ascendant in the Indian community. No longer is the arranged marriage as widespread as it once was and in the urban areas it is almost non-existent. In families in which business considerations, such as large landholdings or a substantial commercial enterprise, once held the extended family together because division of the property between the claimants would have been imprudent, the present tendency is for the business to continue as a unit but for the individual families to maintain their separate existence.

There is a definite tendency for behaviour in this important area to converge. The Indians, Africans and Amerindians are all groups with approaches to family life somewhat different from the Christian nuclear family but the Amerindians only make up about 5 per cent of the population, are mainly locked up in their interior communities and anyhow have lost most of their original family pattern through their lengthy attachment to the Christian churches. The Indians and Africans were the major protagonists and, together with a common view of what constitutes the good life and the best means of attaining it, contemporary developments are leading to a convergence of approach regarding the nuclear family.

Race and class in the post-independence period

While the issue of race has not disappeared, an interesting feature of the post-independence period is the destruction of the old white ruling group and its indigenous supporters and the effect this has had on the ethnic frontier. Once the state passed to the PNC and the process of Guyanization began in earnest it meant that many members of the Coloured, African and Indian middle class who were frustrated by the old ruling group were now promoted to positions they thought rightfully their own. The nationalization process which began in the late 1960s, added momentum to that process.

Particularly destructive to the national section of the old ruling class was the nationalization of external trade in 1970 and the new regime's encouragement and organization of co-operatives and state agencies to take part in internal commercial distribution. With the nationalization of Booker in 1976 the regime became dominant in internal trade. The industrial arm of the national section of the old ruling class was based primarily in external and internal commerce. Those legal and other firms which depended upon it were similarly undercut as the regime began to favour its own supporters. There was nothing left but for this strata to migrate *en masse* to the United States and Canada.

By the late 1970s the PNC had successfully created a new middle class, consisting mainly of its supporters, with its base in government and the nationalized industries. With over 80 per cent of the economy in its hands, the PNC held significant patronage. No other sector of the economy could function satisfactorily without its goodwill and in time that came to be dependent upon the level of support one gave to the regime. The question of race still plagued this middle group for many of the Indians within it still believed that the PNC had no right to power and that it discriminated against them. They pointed to the small number of Indians in the security forces as a concrete example of racial/political discrimination. However, those who took over from the Europeans still perpetuate European traditions, not only in their approach to the family but in all areas of life. Indeed, they had no other frame of reference. One of the criteria for arriving at elite positions was a lengthy period of exposure to European education, with all that that entailed and since this new elite has become the focus of aspiration one could expect to see the continued gradual destruction of traditional patterns of behaviour.

In the immediate post-independence period the African and Coloured sections of this new middle class applauded the PNC, though later developing its own complaints. On the whole these people had supported the PNC because they believed it to be nationalist, anti–communist and anti–Indian. They wanted to be rid of the Europeans and to assume their positions of power and privilege and in the initial period this did occur. Very early on, however, they came to realize that the PNC could not rule without some Indian support for which it had to pay a great deal in patronage. This has been a perpetual bone of contention for the more racist members of the party. However, in the mid–1970s the regime began to show Marxist intiatives and to make attempts to democratize (according to the middle class the correct term would be 'disrupt') the privileged education system, which every member of this class wanted to retain for their children, through such means as zoning and the rotation of teachers. Needless to say, these policies were frustrated but when coupled with the abysmal economic performance which makes it impossible to provide what would appear to be the basic necessities of life one understands why the PNC has now lost the support of this group and must dread the possibility of an alliance between its Indian and African sections.

Guyanization and nationalization have brought some material and psychological benefits to the urban and rural workers but here again the Indians claim that they are discriminated against. For example, some in the rural areas claim that the regime discriminated against their co-operatives in spite of its oft–stated commitment to co-operation. However, the blatant labour exploitation of the pre-independence period no longer exists and with nationalization the closed society of the white managerial staff has become more open through the recruitment of more Guyanese and the deliberate opening up of some of the facilities to the workers. The education system has become somewhat more democratized in that there are free secondary schools in most areas although there are still special facilities of which the middle class may make use. Housing provision has also improved. The hated *logies* (the dilapidated barracks–type buildings in which many of the workers and their families had to live in the most despicable and overcrowded conditions) are no more.

Nevertheless, the relationships of production have not changed in the nationalized industries and from the economic standpoint the workers are still ruthlessly exploited by the new managerial group. The general contention is that this level of exploitation is essential if the process of accumulation and hence the development of the nation is to be hastened. On the other hand, others have complained that the level of incompetence, corruption and high living by the middle class is in direct contradiction to what is prescribed for the workers (Thomas, 1984).

Other policies of the regime, such as the cultural liberalism it encourages, help to create an atmosphere of tolerance. But of course the fact that the PNC came to office as essentially an African party and has since maintained itself there by rather dubious means could hardly enhance racial harmony. One of the major arguments against the plural society model and, to a lesser degree, the Marxists, is that they do not focus sufficiently upon the internal workings of ethnic groups and unless this is done we will not understand any area of PNC ethnic policy. While outsiders tend to look at the Indians as an homogenous group, the various religious underpinnings of their ethnicity make them less homogenous than the Africans. It is true that 84 per cent of them are Hindu but the Muslims have achieved a prominence which far outweighs their numbers and has made the Hindus quite suspicious of them. Furthermore, there is fierce elite competition within each of these sub-groups and by using the resources of the state to support a section of the elite the PNC has been able to gain significant influence over the behaviour of their communities without having any actual grass-roots support.

However, in recent times the regime has found itself in a financial crisis which has led to attempts being made to hold down wages and to the curtailment of the importation of many basic and traditional dietary items for which there are no adequate substitutes. Widespread unemployment among the urban and rural proletariat, shortage of materials and equipment for production and poor incentives for the farmers have contributed to the general frustration. People of all races and all classes in society have gradually come to question the PNC's ability to rule effectively. Thus, in the face of a deep social crisis which threatens to consume the society, there appears on the horizon a unity of race and class against the regime. Whether or not the current situation is the basis of lasting unity or is merely a collective response to a crisis situation, which is likely, as the pluralists have predicted, to break out in violence once the authority of the PNC is weakened, will depend upon the political activities and organizational capabilities of the leading political actors.

4 The Ruling Party

The movement

The breakup of the PPP which at first caused jubilation in the ranks of national and international capital and a significant proportion of the indigenous middle class, soon gave way to consternation as that party proceeded to victory in the 1957 and 1961 elections. Burnham's belief that he would be able to create a national movement, 'which includes all Guianese who agree that we should no longer be a colony' (Payne, 1973, p. 12) was not to be realized. One of his first efforts to create the movement was frustrated when his support for a merger between his faction of the PPP and the UDP was rejected at the Burnhamite Congress of June 1957, just a few months before the first election to be held since the suspension of the 1953 Constitution. Congress turned down the proposal on the grounds that 'Many who now pretend to love this Party and who are anxious to give it respectability do not seem to appreciate that we have principles and that success at the forthcoming elections is not the sole aim of our Party' (*Documentary History*, 1975, p. 23). For the Negro middle class in the UDP, fearful of both communism and the increasing prominence of the Indians, such idealism must have been most alarming, especially since the Burnham faction had won the support of the African working class which made it impossible for the middle class to mobilize a credible opposition to the PPP without it. But, as the Burnhamites were being idealistic, the Jaganites had already criticized the 'ultra left' of his group which Burnham had accused of 'tactless adventurism' and they had left the party at the same time as it began to broaden its base by the infusion of middle-class Indians and business interests.

The Burnhamites were soundly defeated in the 1957 election and the decision not to unite with the UDP is usually viewed as contributing to that defeat. However, the evidence does not suggest such a conclusion. The UDP only won one seat at that election and nowhere was its influence sufficient to have turned the tide against the PPP.

After their defeat the Burnhamites merged with the UDP to form the PNC. A special Congress held in October 1957 adopted the new party name and also changed the name of its propaganda organ from *PPP Thunder* (Burnhamite) to the *New Nation*. Not long after, the YSM and the Women's Auxiliary, renamed the Women's Revolutionary Socialist Movement (WRSM) in 1976, were created as the PNC's youth and women's arms respectively.

At the 1957 Congress Burnham was returned as Leader of the party. J. P. Latchmansingh took Burnham's old PPP position and became Chairman, Eusi Kwayana (Sidney King) was elected First Vice-Chairman with F. A. De Silva Second Vice-Chairman; Jai Narine Singh became General Secretary, Burnham's sister Jessie Burnham and A. L. Jackson were Assistant Secretaries and Stanley Hugh was the Treasurer. These, together with a few other officers, made up the Central Executive Committee (CEC) of the party.

The African and Coloured middle and working classes were united in the PNC but it was not long before the growing influence of the middle class began to worry the old Burnhamites who complained bitterly that middle class opportunism was taking the party off course (Payne, 1973, p. 57). It is noteworthy that the PNC has never been able to significantly extend this base which in recent times has contracted. The election of 1961 demonstrated that the country had become more polarized than ever. The PPP received 88 per cent of the votes which were cast on the plantations while the PNC took 65 per cent of the urban votes (Green, 1974, p. 25); Burnham's hopes of leading a national independence movement were slowly evaporating. He had to find a method of wrenching power from the PPP: proportional representation and coalition with the UF provided the levers. The PNC did not arrive in government as a national revolutionary movement supported by a broad national front. Like the PPP it was racially based but unlike the PPP its programmatic platform was highly anti-communist.

The political character of the PNC

Flushed with its 'victory' at the 1973 election at which it 'won' a two-thirds majority, in November of that year a special Congress of the party decided that the time had arrived for it to assume supremacy over the Government and that it should gear itself to give conceptual and practical leadership in all areas of social life. The special Congress left it to the General Council to redraft the party constitution in keeping with these declared objectives.

Article 1 of the 1974 Constitution declares the party to be a socialist party committed to the tenets of co-operativism. As we shall see in Chapter 8, what exactly is meant by co-operative socialism has changed significantly over time. Article 2 states the objectives of the party, which each member is required to learn and adhere to, as follows:

1. To secure and maintain through the practice of co-operative socialism the interest, well-being and prosperity of all the people of Guyana.
2. To pursue our commitment to the socialist ideal and more particularly to ensure that the people of Guyana own and control for their benefit the natural resources of the country.
3. To provide every Guyanese the opportunity to work for and share in the economic well-being of the country and to ensure that there is equality of opportunity in the political, economic and social life of the country.
4. To motivate the people of Guyana to improve by their own efforts and through the party, the communities in which they live.
5. To pursue constantly the goal of national self-reliance.
6. To work for the closest possible association of Guyana with her Caribbean neighbours and to maintain a link with international organisations and agencies whose aims and objectives are consistent with those of the People's National Congress.
7. To nominate and support members of the Party for elections to the Central Legislature and local government councils. [Party Constitution, 1974]

The 1983 Constitution maintains these objectives but adds that at the present stage of development socialism implies an unremitting and relentless struggle against poverty, ignorance, reaction, imperialism, and so on (Party Constitution, 1983).

The national organization

The basic unit of the party is the Group, which must consist of no less than twelve members. Each year the Group elects its officers: a

Chairman, Secretary and Treasurer and if necessary a Vice-Chairman, Assistant Secretary, Organizing Secretary and no more than three other members. Provisions exist for Groups to be formed at places of employment and in other socio-economic organizations but these are not widespread as there is the obvious difficulty that in a multi-party situation once the PNC allows itself to form such groups other parties would demand similar rights. Groups are therefore mainly residential and in 1983 the General Secretary reported that there were 544 Groups, with an average of 15.2 members.

The national organization of the party is based upon local government demarcations and is said to be organized according to the system of democratic centralism whereby the lower organ elects the one above it but is responsible to the latter for its work. As we will see, this is not a correct definition of how the PNC is organized. Figure 1 gives an indication of the relationship which exists between the party and the local government system.

The People's Co-operative is the smallest local government unit and the structure goes up through the Neighbourhood, Community, District, Sub-Region and Region. When the system is completely established each of these units will be governed by a Council. Presently, only the Regional Councils are established although the geographical demarcation of the units has been completed. It is possible for there to be more than one Group in a People's Co-operative but this is unusual. Group formation and elections must be approved by the Committee above it, which is the People's Co-operative Committee, or when there is no People's Co-operative Committee, the Committee of the tier above. Constitutionally, Group meetings are to be held at least once a month but more frequent meetings are encouraged by the Secretariat.

At present party Conferences are held at Regional, Sub-Regional and District levels and attempts are being made for them to be introduced in the People's Co-operative areas. When the system is properly established annual Conferences will be held for each subdivision and representation to such Conferences will be based upon Group membership. Every Group will be able to send one delegate for every five financial members to each Conference. The YSM and WRSM are entitled to send one delegate for every twenty-five members. Party Members of Parliament (MPs) assigned to the given area and members

Local government demarcations	The party structure
	Biennial Congress
	↑
Regional Councils	Regional Conferences
	↑ Regional Committees
Sub-Regional Councils	Sub-Regional Conferences
	↑ Sub-Regional Committees
District Councils	District Conferences
	↑ District Committees
Community Councils	Community Conferences
	↑ Community Committees
Neighbourhood Councils	Neighbourhood Conferences
	↑ Neighbourhood Committees
People's Co-operative Councils	People's Co-operative Conferences
	↑ People's Co-operative Committees
	Group

Figure 1. National party organization

of the relevant local government district are ex-officio delegates to its Conferences. There are also provisions for organizations affiliated to the party to be represented at such Conferences and all members of Groups within the given area are entitled to attend, but only accredited delegates have a right to speak and vote.

The relevant area Committee—for example the Community Committee within the Community division—must report to Conference on the state of the party and on past and future activities and, except for the People's Co-operative Conferences which are only empowered to elect five members to serve on the People's Co-operative Committee, all Conferences elect two members to serve on its area Committee and an alternate General Council member (the Secretary of each subdivision except the People's Co-operative is the accredited General Council Representative).

Each subdivision is managed by a Committee but, as we have seen, such Committees are only partially elected by the Conferences. The People's Co-operative Conferences elect five committee members whilst the other Conferences elect three, one of whom is the alternative General Council member. Given their different areas, all Committee members are drafted similarly. Thus, the Chairman and Vice-Chairman of a Committee are the Chairman and Vice-Chairman of the relevant local government Council if the party is in control of local government in the area. If the party is not in control of the given local government area the CEC directs the Committees as to which members they should elect Chairman and Vice-Chairman. Other members of the Committees are the Chairmen of the two Committees immediately below them and the YSM and WRSM Chairmen of the given area and those immediately below. For example, the Sub-Regional Committees will consist of: the Chairman and Vice-Chairman of the Sub-Regional local government Council (if the party controls the Council), the Chairman of the District and Community Committees within the Sub-Region, the Sub-Regional and District Chairmen of the YSM and WRSM, the two members elected by Conference and the alternate General Council member also elected by Conference. The Committees are expected to supervise the work of the tiers immediately below them and to see to their effective functioning.

If the party is in control of the relevant local government Council its Committee is expected to be instrumental in formulating the programme which its members will introduce into the Council and to mobilize members and non-members in support of the implementation of that programme. If it is not in control of the given Council, the Committee will co-ordinate with those of its members on the Council to force the implementation of party policy. However, below the levels of Regional Council local government elections have not been held since 1970 and such local government as presently exists below this level functions with a patchwork of elected and nominated members.

It will be obvious that this system has very little to do with what has commonly become known as democratic centralism. It is not simply that the varying Committees are not elected from below but that they are constituted in a manner that is highly undemocratic. If the CEC finds it necessary to direct the members of the Committees as to which members they should elect as Chairmen and Vice-Charimen when the party is not in control of the local government Council in the area, one can only expect that it, not party members, will choose local government councillors and as such the important members of each Committee. The system is thus highly centralized, allowing for a minimum of grass-roots control. There is also another side to this arrangement which should not be overlooked. It makes nonsense of the idea of the supremacy of the party when it is stated in the party's constitution that state officials—in this case local government representatives—whom the party members have no right to choose will be the local leaders of the party. Indeed, we will see how this works itself out now that Burnham has died. Since the President is elected by the majority party in the National Assembly it is not unreasonable to expect that whoever becomes Leader of the majority party will be presented as its candidate for the Presidency but if the local government situation is anything to go by, the individual who takes over as President can make a legitimate constitutional claim to be made automatic Leader of the party.

The various annual Conferences culiminate in the Biennial Delegates' Congress which is said to be the supreme authority of the party. Before 1975 Congresses were annual events. Each Group is entitled to send one delegate for every ten financial members and the YSM and affiliated organizations are entitled to send one delegate for every fifty financial members up to 1,000 members and thereafter one for every 200 members, provided that, in the case of affiliates, every delegate is a party member. The National Executive Committee of the WRSM and three of its members from each region are accredited Congress delegates. All members of the General Council, Party MPs and members of National Congress of Local Democratic Organs are entitled to attend and participate but only the MPs and members of the National Congress have the right to vote by virtue of their office.

The early Congresses were genuine participatory events where the leadership positions were often defeated. The fact that Burnham lost the issue of coalition with the UDP in 1957 indicates that early Congresses were not as contrived as they are now. Such a situation is all but inconceivable today. Most of the early officers were recognized leaders in their own right and saw Burnham, in the words of the official organ of the Burnhamites as: 'the first among equals, not an autocratic monarch' (*Burnhamite Thunder*, 22 June 1975). Prior to 1973 Congress elected most of the party officers including the Leader, Chairman and General Secretary but this power has been gradually withdrawn. The 1974 Constitution gave the Leader the right to select the General Secretary and the 1983 Constitution gives him the right to select all the officers of the party provided he chooses the General Secretary and Deputy Leader from among the fifteen members of the CEC who are elected by Congress.

The highlights of the Congress are still the Leader's presentation and the General Secretary's Report but other members of the hierarchy do make presentations. At the 1981 Congress papers were presented on the international question, the role of the party, Guyana's territorial integrity and production. These are usually discussed in commissions which report back to the plenary session where further discussions take place. Groups wanting to raise questions or present motions for the consideration of Congress are required to send them to the Secretariat some time before the Congress. There are usually too many of these for Congress to discuss them all. They are scrutinized and those considered most important are put to the Congress. Attempts are made to send written answers to those not discussed at Congress. Messages are heard from foreign delegates. In 1981 about forty foreign delegations, ranging from the Democratic Labour Party of Barbados to the Communist Party of the Soviet Union, brought messages of support. Foreign delegates are awarded honorary membership of the PNC and the proceedings are closed with the leader summing up the issues and outcomes as he sees them and giving the delegates their instructions for the coming period.

The General Council and Central Executive Committee

The General Council is the governing body of the party between Congresses and it meets each quarter. It is not elected by Congress and most of its top officers, being the officers of the party, are selected by the Leader. It consists of all the members of the Executive Committee; the

Secretaries of the regional subdivisions, except the People's Co-operatives; Regional Chairmen; the Chairman of the National Congress of Local Democratic Organs; MPs; three representatives from the YSM; the Chairman of the WRSM and one representative from each affiliate. For some sessions, important state functionaries are invited. The Council listens to addresses and reports from the Leader, General Secretary and others. What appears an inordinate amount of time is spent in discussing reports from the Regional Chairmen and in dealing with what amounts to little more than complaints from rank and file members. Though democratically admirable, this sort of open reporting and discussion can be highly embarrassing and tends to lead to selected reporting, which becomes very evident as the discussions proceed. In the 1980 reorganization it was suggested that before each Council meeting or Congress each of the Executive Secretaries, with the aid of a committee of the General Council, should thoroughly scrutinize state and party activities which are assigned to his/her Department and provide a report which could then be discussed. It was thought that such a procedure would lead to a more frank and objective analysis of difficulties and shortcomings but the idea was not accepted.

From the General Council we come to the Central Executive Committee which in theory is responsible to both Congress and the General Council but, as in all such arrangements, in practice controls both. Before the constitutional changes of 1983, this body consisted of the officers of the party and seven members elected by the General Council from among its members. It is now made up of the Leader and fifteen members elected by the Congress. It has the power to co-opt other persons to its ranks. At any one time the CEC could have as many as thirty members. Its functions as laid down in the constitution are to:

1. Draw up the Party's general programme in conformity with the general policy formulated by Congress.
2. Prepare the agenda for General Council meetings, report on the activities of the Party at each meeting of the General Council and propose a programme for the ensuing period.
3. Implement the decisions and policy of the General Council.
4. Exercise all the rights and fulfill all the duties and obligations of the

General Council between meetings of the Council, and initiate any action in keeping with the general policy of the Party.

5. Receive and take appropriate action on reports from the regional and other Committees and from advisers.
6. Give guidance and direction on general Party policy and on specific issues from time to time.
7. (Have) the power to summon a meeting of the General Council whenever it deems such a meeting to be necessary.
8. Nominate such subcommittees to carry out such duties and assignments as it may consider necessary from time to time.

This most important body of the party is constitutionally obliged to meet at least once a month but it usually meets twice monthly, at one time to discuss policy issues and at the other to consider administrative issues. Policy papers provided by its members, the Secretariat, Ministers or other advisers, or issues raised by any of its members, can provide the basis for discussion and there is normally a free and frank airing of views at the end of which the Leader sums up the discussion and lays down the policy as he sees it. There is little doubt that fundamental decisions are made without the CEC's knowledge. A good example is that relating to the introduction of free education which only reached CEC members by way of the mass media.

The officers of the party

The 1974 Constitution provides for the following officers of the Party: the Leader, Deputy Leader, Chairman, First and Second Vice-Chairmen, General Secretary, Assistant General Secretary, Executive Secretaries, Treasurer, Co-Treasurer and Editor of *New Nation*. The 1983 Constitution does not change this position although the Leader is now the only officer of the Party who is actually elected by the membership and he chooses all the others, some of whom must be drawn from a list of fifteen CEC members elected by Congress.

This is worth noting, for the Leader is the one officer who it is constitutionally impossible to remove. He has some rather formidable reserve powers. Article 22 of the Constitution states that:

If the Leader in his deliberate judgement is of the opinion that a situation of emergency has arisen in the Party, he shall have power, notwithstanding any provisions in the Rules, on giving written notice to the General Secretary of his opinion, to take all action that he may in his absolute direction consider necessary to correct such a situation, and for this purpose he may assume and exercise any or all of the powers of the Biennial Delegates Congress, the General Council, the Central Executive Committee, any other Committee, Group, Arm, Organ or of any officer or official of the Party. [Party Constitution, 1983, pp. 64–5]

Furthermore,

If the General Council, the Central Executive Committee or the Administrative Committee has not been constituted or for any reason cannot function, the Leader may exercise all or any of its powers or may authorize such members as he may deem fit to exercise its powers for the time being. [Ibid.]

Perhaps these provisions were designed to prevent the recurrence of the devious intra-party manoeuvres which preceded the split of the PPP in 1955 and in which Burnham was a prime mover, but whatever the reasons for their introduction they make it impossible for one to classify the PNC as a democratic party. Once the affairs of the Party are proceeding in a direction which suits the Leader, a semblance of justice and fairplay will be maintained; otherwise the Leader can be expected to use his unlimited constitutional authority. The only obstacle in his way is the written document he must present to the General Secretary informing him of his decision. However, when one considers that the Leader appoints the General Secretary, that provision is, in the words of Thomas Jefferson in reference to the impeachment provisions of the American Constitution, 'not even a scarecrow'. Indeed, since the Party cannot be constitutionally removed from office and since its Leader is in effect Leader for life, what really exists in Guyana is a life presidency.

Between 1974 and 1984 Dr Ptolomy A. Reid held the offices of Deputy Leader and General Secretary and once Burnham had elevated himself to the Presidency in 1980, Reid also became Prime Minister. Through the changes which took place in 1984 Reid kept his position of Deputy Leader but Desmond Hoyte became Prime Minister and Ranji Chandisingh (one-time Executive member and chief Marxist theorist of the PPP who crossed the floor in 1976) took up the position of General Secretary. The constitution states that the General Secretary will be in charge of the Party Secretariat and be responsible for its effective operation. Together with the Leader, Deputy Leader and Chairman, the General Secretary is an ex-officio member of all committees and arms of the Party. The 1974 Constitution introduced a new kind of Secretariat. The new organization was called the Office of the General Secretary of the PNC and the Ministry of National Development. For the first time an attempt was made to create a working relationship between a government ministry and a political party. The problems which arose were enormous.

The Secretariat

The 1974 Secretariat was divided into five Departments. The Office of the General Secretary proper included the Permanent Secretary, who is the legal head of a normal government ministry. The Permanent Secretary was in charge of actual ministry personnel, administration and finance. He had no control over party matters, which fell to four Executive Secretaries, each with the rank of a Minister of State. The hybrid created by putting the party office and a ministry together was constitutionally necessary if the work of the Secretariat was to be financed by the state. By law, the Permanent Secretary is the responsible financial officer of a ministry, so it was necessary to have a Permanent Secretary in the Office of the General Secretary if public funds were to be obtained.

It was generally believed that, for its programme of socialism to succeed, the Party had to implement a major programme of mobilization and education to raise consciousness and make the population aware of its objectives. It would have been unreasonable to expect Party members to pay for this increased emphasis on mobilization and training and the task of the Secretariat was to do precisely that. It mobilized the nation for all manner of events and ran courses, such as the Developers' Programme, intended to explain the socialist direction of the PNC to a wide range of people, which included government and party officers and members. It also attempted to work out as clearly as possible many of the conceptual difficulties which developed with the new socialist emphasis. For example, it tried to create a unity between Marxism and co-operativism and to indicate how it was to be applied in Guyana.

In some ways the party suffered as a result of these increasing activities. In April 1973 it had 50,000 members (Burnham, 1975, p. 49), but only a small fraction of these were active. (Indeed, part of the reason for demanding a better quality member was to force this large inactive section to become more involved at a time when the PNC appeared to have had all the answers. However, rather than succumbing to the new demands, most members left the Party and by 1978 its membership had fallen to 15,000.) The number of active members was too small for the strain that the new Secretariat placed upon it and it buckled. There was constant pressure upon the same section of people to organize, to march, to do community work, to attend courses, etc. This led to widespread disillusionment, particularly when one considers that there were no significant personal benefits to be gained from such activities and that people who were much more prosperous and appeared to be obtaining more benefits from the PNC were not visibly involved in such events.

Of course, some short-term benefits accrued through the funding which was made available by the state. The Party became much more visible and organized and, although the membership base was decreasing at an alarming rate, it gave the impression of invincibility which drew many people of all classes closer to it. Also, of necessity, the education programmes contained a party bias since it was the policy of the party which was to be implemented by the government of the day. However, even here a bureaucracy—which one grass-roots' member called a 'partocracy'—developed, the existence of which seemed to depend upon circulating a superabundance of paper. This was particularly noticeable to the older members whose attachment to the party was based upon emotional ties which the new partocrats tried to understand but could not compute. This also contributed to the fall-off in membership.

The other four Departments of the 1974 Office of the General Secretary were those of Planning and Research, Finance, Administration and Regional Affairs and Public Welfare. The Department of Planning and Research tried to initiate and systematically formulate the programme of the Party. It also became involved in party foreign relations, printed authorized literature and did many other odd jobs. Through the Permanent Secretary and the party Treasurer, the Department of Finance took care of the different Secretariat activities and the Department of Administration was expected to service the Secretariat and see that the local groups were adequately administered. It was also responsible for the acquisition and preparation of buildings, equipment and venues for the different activities. Finally, there was the Department of Regional Affairs and Public Welfare which actually monitored and organized national and local events through the party and other social organizations. It was also responsible for membership.

Business did not proceed smoothly. This was largely due to the innovative nature of the arrangement, the fact that it was top-heavy, with insufficient work to go round, and the ambitions of the people who were thrown together. The Permanent Secretary was in a daze as to his/her relationship with the different Departments. In a normal ministry he/she is the head with whom the different heads of department have to consult. In the Office of the General Secretary no such relationship existed; the different Departments were ruled by people with the status of Ministers of Government who were theoretically superior to the Permanent Secretary. Before long some Departments were creaming off the work of others, claiming that they were incompetent, although on some occasions, one suspected political strategy was involved. Thus, the Department of Planning and Research took over the servicing of important party committees from the Department of Administration. Rifts among the Executive Secretaries, particularly with relation to seniority, made it possible for the Permanent Secretary to eventually undercut them. Such behaviour is not unexpected in most newly created organizations of this kind but what is more to the point is that this party organization had no direct connection with the functions of state officials. The Secretaries were not closely concerned with the formulation and monitoring of state policy as in the classical communist party; they were essentially concerned with party activities and with propaganda and mobilization.

By 1978 the Secretariat was disintegrating, as a few powerful Party officers intended it to. At the weekly meetings of the Administrative Committee (which, according to the party constitution, is responsible for planning and supervising the day-to-day activities of the Secretariat and is chaired by the General Secretary and consists of such other officers as he believes necessary) the weaker Departments were harassed. In the eyes of those officers the Secretariat was becoming a hotbed of subversives. What was more to the point was that elements in the organization took the socialist content of the Declaration of Sophia too seriously and, more importantly, began to show sympathy for closer links with the PPP. So worried was this opportunistic element, who knew that the equation in Chapter 2 would be endangered by such moves, that an attempt was made in 1976 to pass a motion at the CEC that the PNC would never merge with the PPP. Since the Secretaries were busy quarrelling with each other they delighted in outside attacks on their colleagues, failing to recognize the underlying destructive intentions.

By the second half of the 1970s the economic situation began to bite and cuts in government spending had to be made all round. The top-heavy Secretariat, which the opposition spared no opportunity of attacking, accusing the regime of using government funds for party purposes, was an obvious target. In fairness, economies could have been made but, as it turned out, national economic management was in the hands of the very people who considered the Secretariat subversive and they used that leverage to curtail its activities. However, the final blow came with the impending election of 1978.

With the exception of the General Secretary, Dr P. A. Reid, the people in control of the Departments of the Secretariat had no political base. They were quarrelling with each other, they had drawn the wrath of senior and important people and had alienated the grass-roots members with their plethora of bureaucratic procedures and highbrow ideology. It would have been extremely unwise to place the delicate operations of election management, particularly in the unique circumstances of Guyana, in the hands of such people. Given the specific context of the organization, these people were not particularly ineffective but their infighting and failure to grasp the overall picture made it possible for their enemies to spotlight their defects. As a result, a Minister of State, whom the Party leaders believed was more in touch with the real world, was appointed to the Secretariat to assist the General Secretary. He proceeded to use all the power of the General

Secretary *vis-à-vis* the Executive Secretaries, who complained that supremacy of the Party, as outlined in the Declaration of Sophia, was being undermined when a Minister of State was allowed to dominate party officers. Thus was further discord introduced into the system. In 1979, the Secretariat was destroyed by a fire which the PNC claimed was started by members of the WPA. However, by that time it was little more than an election campaign office.

The introduction of the 1980 Constituion, the completion of the election process, the destruction and rebuilding of the party head-quarters and the deepening economic and social crisis meant that the depleted Secretariat had to be re-organized. For financial reasons the new Secretariat remained attached to the Ministry of National Development but an attempt was made to distinguish as clearly as possible the work of the two institutions. The Secretariat now had six departments: Finance, Administration, Education and Research, Economic and International Affairs, Regional Affairs and Public Welfare and Field Activities. What was significant about this new arrangement was that the new Departments were to concern themselves with party work as well as to monitor government activities to see that party policy was being implemented.

If the Department of Education and Research is taken as an example, its party tasks were to see to the effective implementation of party propaganda, particularly among party members and to maintain a research section capable of supporting the other Secretariat Departments and organs of the party. At the level of the state the Department was responsible for monitoring technical, vocational, primary, secondary and higher education. It was also to see to it that party policy was followed in the areas of culture, scholarships, and information. There was to be no *ad hoc* interference in state institutions but the CEC organized subcommittees which included the party Secretary concerned to help with the task of monitoring.

The system came to nothing for several reasons. State positions are more prestigious than party offices. This is not difficult to under-stand: Guyanese are culturally accustomed to the political values of the West where state functions and functionaries are more important than party ones. Secondly, most people in the country who hold senior and prestigious state positions are not members of political parties so they do not wish this relationship to change, which would certainly happen if party officers were allowed to effectively monitor and report on state activities. Thirdly, barring the weekly Cabinet meetings, ministerial appointees are free of any popular and detailed scrutiny and the introduction of an effective monitoring system could be extremely onerous. Thus we have a coalition of top party and state functionaries willing and able to frustrate such projects. As a result of these influences and the general ambivalence of Burnham who seemed to enjoy his state positions much more than his party ones, the subcommittees organized by the CEC to carry out the monitoring were put in charge of the very people whom they were supposed to monitor, i.e. the Ministers.

In 1984, the Departments of the Secretariat were once again re-arranged but the breadth of their operations was not changed. There are now Departments of National Production, Financial Administration and Economic Projects, Party Affairs and Mass Organizations, Personnel Administrative Services, National Orientation and International Relations, and Maintenance and Welfare. These are all situated in the new Secretariat building in Sophia, Georgetown and the same financial relationship with the Ministry of National Development remains.

Membership

There are seven classes of party membership. Child membership is open to children up to 14 years of age whose parents or guardians are members of the Party. At the last Biennial Congress in 1983 the General Secretary reported that there were only 607 child members. Youth membership for those between the ages of 14 and 35 operates via the YSM but on reaching 18 they may apply for adult membership. In the 1960s and early 1970s the YSM was much more vibrant than it is today. The 1983 report claimed that it had a membership of only 357. This is incredible for a ruling party of a country where, according to its own estimates, 60 per cent of the population is below the age of 25, (*Speakers Brief*, 1980, p. 6). The most able youths were never to be found within the ranks of the YSM but today the situation is worse than ever. Those close to the YSM accept that opportunist elements are rife, intending to use the movement as a stepping stone to top government and bureaucratic positions. Not surprisingly, in his 1983 report the General Secretary recommended that the YSM adopt the slogan 'do' to inspire it to greater activity and he warned that in the coming years the organization would have to 'concentrate its efforts in strengthening its popular base by active mobilisation of the youths of Guyana in every sector. . . . establishing itself as the true vanguard, ready to defend the gains of our revolution' (General Secretary's Address, 1983, p. 9).

At the age of 18 any Guyanese may apply to become an adult member of the party. To be accepted, the individual must be sponsored by at least two members, be a member of a co-operative society, pay membership fees, subscribe to the *New Nation* and, if eligible, be a member of a trade union. The aspirant member is also required to purchase and read the party constitution and such other works that may from time to time be designated essential reading by the General Council. The new member is accepted on probation of not less than one year before he/she is allowed youth or adult membership. Only the Leader of the Party or the CEC has the right to reduce the probationary period. Membership is only available through a local Group. If the executive of the Group concludes that the probationary period has not been satisfactorily served the period may be extended for another term or the individual may be declared unsuited for membership. To satisfactorily fulfil the terms of probation the individual must have accepted and conform to the principles and programme of the party. This can mean anything from simply subscribing to the *New Nation*, attending Group meetings and contributing financially to the party to actually selling *New Nation*, doing community work or breaking strikes which are defined as 'political' by the party. Once the probationary period has been satisfactorily completed the individual should receive full membership but in reality most people continue year after year as probationary members, there being only a small core of full members. The process by which one becomes a full member is not well-known and one gets the impression that this is deliberately kept vague. Furthermore, many people avoid full membership because full members are expected to make heavy financial contributions to the numerous party activities.

In 1983 the total adult membership, full and probationary, of this party which claims to be the vanguard of the revolution, was about 1 per cent of the population: 8,300—a far cry from the 50,000 members it boasted in 1973. Figures are not usually provided as to the social composition of this membership but there is little doubt that it is still dominated by Africans, although one gets the impression that, unlike the earlier days, most of them are rural people. The urban base of the party has largely dissipated: its *de facto* control of government makes it possible for it to call on the support of a significant section of the middle class when it needs to but most of these people are not party members and are not found at party group meetings.

As we have seen, a significant fall in membership occurred after 1974 and was partly the result of some conceptual and practical errors on the part of the leadership as they attempted to create a disciplined vanguard party in inappropriate conditions. After 1974 every effort was made to infuse the party with a high level of discipline. Strict adherence to the rule that people must be members of the Group in their place of residence and an emphasis upon the quality and not the quantity of the membership was introduced. Burnham never tired of insisting that, 'Party membership must be a reward to be sought after,a qualification which has to be earned. It must not be come by, unless the applicant has gone through the crucible of training, testing and performance. It cannot, I repeat, cannot be bought.' (Burnham, 1974, p. 14.) This pronouncement was made in the heady days of 1974 when the party looked invincible: Burnham could not tell what the future would hold.

The constitution states that persons are to be members of Groups in the areas in which they live but the General Secretary and People's Co-operative Committee have the authority to make exceptions for a limited number of reasons. Particularly in the urban areas, where the PNC had the bulk of its support when this policy was first introduced, it caused great dismay among the party faithful who had built up and maintained close relationships with Groups which they continued to attend after they had left the area. The new Secretariat, organized after 1974, set about outlining clearly which Group members in a given area should attend and many of those who were obliged to leave their old Group did not bother to rejoin.

Secondly, the stress which Burnham placed upon the quality of membership was certainly not sensible in a multi-party situation where the votes of all have equal value. Even if the party manipulates the electoral process it needs to have a significant membership base if only to demonstrate its broad-based support. However, we should remember that this statement was made at a time when it appeared to the leadership that the PNC had all the answers and many people were moving closer to the party. Of course this movement was not as great as it appeared to the leadership and the Groups were never in a position to turn away members. When the bad times arrived in the late 1970s and the debates began as to the efficacy of trying to impose this type of discipline in the context of Guyana it was largely theoretical and a relaxation of the process could not forestall the reality of falling membership.

Thirdly, party membership was a burden which demanded endless financial contributions and made calls upon the individual's time. The general impression that membership led to employment was only marginally true. Most of the senior people in the state sector where the jobs existed were not party members and looked askance at the employment of people who, because of their access to the political leadership, could easily become troublesome. These managers had the backing of Article 9 of the constitution which states that, 'No member shall tender, display or otherwise use his party card to gain himself or any other person, any benefit or favour or otherwise improperly to influence any person or agency.' In any case, by the late 1970s the economic situation had become so severe that far from employing party members it was they who had to face the brunt of the retrenchment programme which resulted from the IMF dictate that the public bureaucracy be pruned. Many managers used this opportunity to rid themselves of troublemakers.

It is recommended that the female members of the party should join the WRSM; most, however, did not. In 1983 the General Secretary reported that the WRSM had only 825 members although one would never suspect that its membership was so small from its high visibility in the urban areas. The 1983 Constitution now states that women members 'shall' be organized in the WRSM. The popular base of the present organization cannot even approximate to that of its predecessor which, with fewer resources, was at one time thought to be better organized than the party. In its heyday the Women's Auxiliary was said to form the backbone of the party. This pivotal role of women within the African-dominated PNC should come as no surprise given our understanding of the matrifocal nature of Afro-Guyanese communities. So pervasive was the influence of women in the PNC that such prominent leaders as Kwayana complained of what he termed the 'petticoat faction' of middle-class women with inordinate influence over the leadership (Payne, 1973, p. 59). The members of the Women's Auxiliary saw their role as striving to raise the political consciousness of men and women. To that end they organized rallies, lectures, numerous kinds of fundraising activities and campaigned from house to house. Like the WRSM, they operated within the ideological and organization framework set by the party and it would be difficult to overestimate the contribution they made to the eventual victory of the PNC.

However, one should bear in mind that in discussing the Women's Auxiliary we are discussing a mass movement which was fired by nationalism, ethnicity and anti-communism. Together with the organizational dictates of the post-1974 Secretariat, the new ideological orientation towards the much more formalistic doctrines of Marxist/Leninism, which did not easily give rise to emotional attachments and which was in direct contradiction to what the movement had struggled for, drove many of this old guard from the party. By the time its designation changed in January 1976, the organization consisted of a few old stalwarts, many of whom held one of its offices and a small group of younger people attracted by the new socialist orientation. But even among these young people much of the original zest has now evaporated, although this is hidden by the large amount of resources the organization has at its disposal.

The chairman of the WRSM is Viola Burnham, the widow of the former President, and this has opened avenues which, under normal conditions, might have remained closed. In 1984 the WRSM received financial and other aid from international organizations such as the Inter-American Development Bank, UNICEF and the Commonwealth Fund, while the resources of national institutions such as the Guyana Co-operative Agricultural and Industrial Development Bank, and a wide range of other organizations were expected to contribute to its projects. In 1984 it was involved in approximately twenty different development projects (Project Report of the WRSM, 1984, p. 2).

Affiliated party membership is open to trade unions, co-operative societies and such other organizations as the CEC believes to hold objectives consistent with those of the party. In 1983 there were nineteen affiliates, ranging from the Public Service and General Workers' Union, the Guyana Teachers' Association, the Burma Consumers' Co-operative Society and the Guyana Association of Local Authorities. These organizations are expected to orientate and mobilize their members in support of the party. Finally, there are associate and honorary classes of membership. The former is given to those who accept the platform of the party but for some reason cannot be members and the latter is usually conferred by the CEC or the Leader on foreign delegates who attend Congress.

Discipline

One of the most persistent complaints of the opposition concerns the level of corruption which is said to exist in official circles. Most Guyanese would accept that there is a problem, and, appearing to bend to this wave of opinion, in 1974 the Declaration of Sophia provided a 'Code of Conduct' for party members and leaders (Burnham, 1974, pp. 33–5). It designated the following people as leaders: the President, the Prime Minister; Ministers of the Government; the Attorney General; PNC Members of Parliament; party officers as defined under Article 14 of the party constitution; such other office-holders as the General Council of the party may from time to time add to this list and the spouses and children under 18 years of age of any of the above.

The first section of the Code states that party members shall not ask for or accept any gift or money for any action done or not done as a result of membership of the party. The burden of proof rests upon the acceptor of such a gift to demonstrate that it does not fall within certain prohibited categories. Members are also prohibited from using party property for their personal benefit without the permission of the General Secretary.

According to Section 2 of the Code, party leaders should not hold stocks or directorships in private companies unless they were nominated to do so by the party or government. A party leader is also prevented from renting land or dwelling houses without the permission of the Leader. A leader cannot engage in private business unless he works in it himself and employs no more than ten persons. Within one month of appointment, leaders are required to submit to the Leader a sworn written statement of all the assets and liabilities they, their spouses and their unmarried children under the age of 18 hold and where such assets and liabilities are situated.

Such statements were usually submitted but many party leaders have been substantially involved in private business. One must assume that they received the dispensation of the Leader. Furthermore, this sort of Code is of limited use if party leaders decide to send their illicit funds abroad. The issue of corruption has not gone away: if anything, it has become more widespread, and in recognition of that fact, in his address to the first session of the Supreme Congress of the People, Burnham recalled that the 1981 party Congress had recommended and that his government had acted upon the recommendation that an Accountability Committee be appointed to 'ferret out all cases of corruption whether they were in breach of the present law or not' (Burnham, 1982, p. 8). He said that the formal legislation which was required to give teeth to the Committee was in draft and promised to, 'submit it to this Congress for your perusal, comment and recommendations' (ibid). What happened to that law is not certain but nothing was heard of it in Burnham's second (1983) or third (1984) address to the Supreme Congress.

Whether or not the Accountability Committee is locked in investigations of great national significance is not public knowledge but at the 1983 Congress the issue of corruption and indiscipline was still worrying the General Secretary. In his address he threatened party members with Article 23 of the constitution which makes provision for the appointment of a party Disciplinary Committee. 'I suggest that all party members, new and old, should begin to study or review this article diligently' (General Secretary's Address, 1983, p. 8). Perhaps that process is also continuing!

5 Constitutional Arrangements

Burnham was not satisfied with the compromises the PNC had to make to come to power and win independence. In 1968 he rid himself of one of these compromises when he returned to office without the help of the United Force (UF). During the 1974 Congress of the PNC, at which Burnham outlined the party's socialist objectives and the decision to change the party's constitution so that it could be re-organized along socialist lines, he made the following announcement with relation to the national Constitution: 'The drafting and sub-sequent promulgation of a new Constitution will, therefore, be under-taken shortly, that is from January 1975. This is a project in which the Party, the public and finally the Parliament will be fully and openly involved' (Burnham, 1974, p. 19).

Burnham pointed to three occasions on which the 1966 Independ-ence Constitution, by which the country was governed until 1980, had proved inadequate and had to be altered to suit prevailing conditions. The 1966 Constitution, drawn up under the watchful eye of British Conservatism, provided special safeguards against the expropriation of private property. As a result, when the PNC sought to nationalize the bauxite industry in 1969 it had to seek the support of the PPP to get the two-thirds parliamentary majority it needed to do so. Burnham was never tired of stating that the Marxist Jagan, 'haggled about how many thousands he should be given to run his office [Office of the Leader of the Opposition] before he agreed to support the government' (Burn-ham, 1980, pp. 18–19).

The PNC refers to 1973 as the year of the 'breakthrough' and it is easy to understand why. In the election of that year, the party allocated to itself 37 of the 53 seats in the House of Assembly, thus taking posses-sion of the two-thirds majority it needed to make certain important constitutional changes. Immediately before the 1973 election, a group of lawyers, worried by a statement from the Women's Auxiliary that the time was 'ripe for a one-party state', was given assurances by Burnham that his party did intend to make constitutional changes but not to set up a one-party state. After the 1973 election, secure in the fact that voting no longer mattered, the PNC changed the constitution to reduce the voting age to 18. The PPP thus gained one of the demands it had made in the pre-independence discussions. The PNC argues that a free and independent people must make its own decisions and learn from its own errors. Thus, told by Burnham that his party intended to remove the Privy Council as the country's final court of appeal, the group of lawyers mentioned above proclaimed:

As lawyers in an independent territory we must understand the view point that it is inconsistent with independence that a final determinant of these matters which finally reach the Privy Council should continue in that body. It is more realistic that we should be able to find such judicial determinant within the areas of the Caribbean including Guyana. [*Mirror*, April, 1978, p. 1]

Quite apart from the fact that so far no such Caribbean court has been established, this statement fails to highlight the central issue of the debates relating to constitutional changes in Guyana. Once a government cannot be legally removed from office, even with the best of constitutional safeguards, the degree of freedom which exists depends upon the sufferance of that government and such a condition is incompatible with a free society. The opponents of constitutional change in Guyana are not usually against the development of independent indigenous institutions: they are against constitutional changes which at best would increase the degree of control the regime has over the population and at worst could lead to large-scale legal repression. Unless this fact is understood the disputes cannot be properly placed in context.

The purpose of a new constitution

Burnham mentioned three occasions on which the 1966 constitution had had to be amended to fulfil the aspirations of his party but there were deeper philosophical issues underlying the introduction of the 1980 Constitution. The task of piloting the Bill through Parliament was left to one of its chief architects, the Attorney General and Minister of Justice, Dr Mohamed Shahabbuddeen, and his presentation to the 1979 PNC Congress provides the backcloth for our analysis.

Shahabbuddeen argued that the 1966 Constitution is what is known as the 'Westminster export type constitution', 'which in themselves are neither good or bad' (Hoyte and Shahabbuddeen, 1979, p. 33). According to the Attorney General, whether or not such constitutions are appropriate to a given situation depends upon that situation. This is meaningless since constitutions are only deemed good or bad in relation to their environment, and the burden of the PNC's contention and all of what Dr Shahabbuddeen had to say was intended to demonstrate that the 1966 Constitution was not good for Guyana. However, the bulk of the Attorney General's argument is devoted to two related issues: Westminster-type constitutions of the kind introduced in 1966 are capitalist orientated documents which make only limited provision for involving the masses in the political process.

The Attorney General argued that the concept of the state enshrined in the 1966 Constitution limits the role of government to setting the parameters within which private economic forces are allowed to operate according to the laws of supply and demand. The hero of such arrangements is the capitalist and the freedoms and liberties which are given priority in such constitutions are those which support the capitalist system. He pointed to the right to own private means of production which is made sacrosanct under such constitutions and argued that when applied to countries like Guyana such constitutions, 'carry with them the right to prompt payment of adequate compensation at current market values. That principle offers no set-off to a newly independent state for the extent to which its natural and human resources might have been exploited during the colonial period by expatriate concerns' (ibid., p. 34). Since countries such as Guyana lack the finance to offer adequate payment for property they wish to repossess they must remain in capitalist economic shackles. It is argued that Guyana found itself in that situation when it attempted to nationalize the bauxite industry.

But while we have amended that clause to break the economic shackles of the past, it is necessary to go on to completion of the whole process by stating explicitly in the constitution itself that property is for social use and is not intended to be ever again used as an instrument of exploitation of man by man. [Ibid., pp. 34–5.]

This is another of those baffling statements. From the 1966 Constitution (amended to facilitate nationalization) the central determinant as to whether or not one remained in economic shackles depended upon whether one had the political will to nationalize with limited compensation, without compensation or had the finance to make adequate payment. The new constitution does not change this situation. Article 142(1) states that:

No property of any description shall be compulsorily taken possession of, and no interest in or right over property of any description shall be compulsorily acquired, except by or under the authority of a written law which provides for compensation for the property or any interest in or right over property so possessed or acquired and either fixes the amount of compensation or specifies the principles on which the compensation is to be determined and given and no such law shall be called in question in any court on the grounds that the compensation provided by law is not adequate.

This means that the regime has the power to offer compensation which takes into consideration the extent to which the resources of the nation have already been exploited by private owners. However, this would be of limited practical use in the future. The nation already controls 80 per cent of the economy and the other 20 per cent is in the hands of co-operatives and small and medium-size private undertakings which are owned by Guyanese. Nothing significant is left to be nationalized and the Guyana Investment Code states categorically that:

As a general rule, where the State is involved, the level of equity participation will be determined on the basis of *negotiations and mutual agreement prior to establishment of the enterprise* and where in an exceptional case the State allows participative investment in a 'Strategic' activity, the participants will agree *prior to its establishment*, on the structure of the enterprise, on mechanisms for changing that structure and relationship between the participants and on the time frame for effecting such changes. [*Investment Code*, 1979, p. 24; italics added.]

Before proceeding with the main argument it is useful to note that 'strategic' activities are defined as those 'which are deemed fundamental to economic development as opposed to current economic survival' (ibid., p. 17). Therefore, the Investment Code continues, 'Strategic Activities implies that it is not possible to prepare a listing, invariant for all times, of the activities which merit the definition

"Strategic'" (ibid., p. 18). If this is so it might prove somewhat difficult to decide on the degree and nature of participation in such industries 'prior to their establishment'! Be that as it may, one would expect that adequate compensation in the event of nationalization would be top priority in any negotiations to establish industries in a country with a record for nationalization such as Guyana. Therefore, for practical purposes, the constitutional statement that property is for social use in no way prevents the payment of adequate compensation: it leaves the nation in precisely the same situation as it was prior to the introduction of the 1980 constitution.

Shahabbuddeen then turned to the role of labour and argued that the constitutional institutionalization of equality 'from each according to his ability, to each according to his work' made clear the regime's commitment to the removal of social inequality. No concrete claim outside the notion of 'commitment' was made here and we suggest that the statement concerning the social use of property should be viewed similarly. Finally, the Attorney General went through the stock criticisms of capitalist society, stating that it does not offer sufficient political and economic participation to the people. Accordingly, the new constitution is intended to do just that: it recognizes the need for government to intervene in society to provide the people with a steadily improving standard of living and participation in decision-making at all levels.

Constitutional controversy

The PNC's contention that it was introducing the new constitution because the old one was inadequate was denied by the opposition. The Marxist PPP challenged the regime to 'define the areas in which it had been obstructed by the constitution.' The PNC could not meet this challenge and indeed the three occasions identified by Burnham only served to demonstrate that the PNC had never come upon a major constitutional obstacle.

On 1st April 1978 the PNC introduced its Constitutional (Amendment) Bill into the National Assembly and the controversy began. The bill sought to amend Article 73 of the 1966 Constitution which laid down the procedure for amending certain provisions of the Constitution. Some of the provisions which were to be affected were those dealing with the protection of fundamental rights and freedoms, elections to and composition of the National Assembly and the Elections Commission. The regime was vague as to which sections of the Constitution it intended to change and many people saw the bill as the beginning of the end of what political freedom was left in Guyana. A significant section of the legal profession claimed that the Bill 'aimed to destroy democracy as we know it', and proceeded to give a dozen reasons why it should be opposed. Among their arguments was the one that 'The referendum seeks to deprive the people of their right to approve or disapprove any new constitution' (Referendum, 1978, p. 70).

The opposition PPP provided a more elaborate and detailed explanation of the PNC's action. By the proposed amendment the PNC intended to postpone elections and legally entrench itself in office indefinitely. Jagan felt so strongly about the issue that he overturned his table in the National Assembly. According to the PPP, 1977 began with an economic crisis of 'devastating proportions' and they estimated that the PNC had lost the support of 75 per cent of the people. Faced with such problems, the government had to be prepared to either hold and rig elections or postpone them. The former was not acceptable and the PPP provided seven reasons why it was not. The shameful shadow of the rigged 1968 and 1973 elections was still in the air and to rig a new election against the tested democratic forces which had developed in the country would have done irreparable damage to the socialist image the regime was building for itself and would have isolated it from progressive international forces. Even if the PNC had turned right again the human rights posture of the Carter administration meant that it could only expect tepid support from that quarter. Furthermore, organizationally, the PNC was falling apart, making it difficult for it to put its rigging machine into top gear. New dynamic forces, such as the WPA, had sprung up in areas which traditionally supported the PNC and the credibility of the PPP was at an all-time high. Finally, many formally marginal political sections of society, such as the churches, wanted political peace (*Mirror*, April, 1978, pp. 2–3).

On 10 July 1978 the PNC destroyed this entire analysis, it mobilized its electoral machine and at the end of the day, without any concern for internal or external forces, it claimed that 71.45 per cent of the electorate had turned up at the polls and voted in its referendum and that 97.7 per cent had voted in favour of its proposals. The Committee of Concerned Citizens which monitored the referendum reported: 'The turn-out of persons estimated by monitors of the Citizens Committee, allowing every possible benefit of doubt, could not have exceeded 15%. If we suppose everyone who voted also cast two proxy votes [the legal maximum], this still does not exceed a 45% turn-out' (Referendum, 1978, p. 10).

The reason why the PPP and so many others are usually wrong about the motivations of the PNC is that they refuse to place most of the top party leaders in the correct political context. The numerous manoeuvres of the PNC tend to confuse their opponents: the WPA denounce it as an anti-socialist dictatorship while the PPP sees a group who could be pushed in a socialist direction. To truly understand the PNC one must understand the varying dimensions of the framework outlined in Chapter 2. It must be allowed that those who matter in the PNC are socialist orientated individuals who believe that their cause will be best served by properly assessing the drift of geopolitical forces. An element of this opportunism is evident from the very early utterances of Burnham. Consider this 1961 statement:

It is clear that one thing we must achieve is national independence, because so long as we are inhabitants of a colony the ultimate power, political, economic and military, remains with those who rule from outside. Socialism will mean a complete change of our present system. Even though we may make gains from time to time and there may come some improvements and reforms, we can never establish socialism in a colony. In the same way when we want to build a house we must lay the foundation; if we want to build socialism we must lay the foundation of national independence. [Burnham, 1970, p. 4]

At first sight this seems a plausible and practical statement, and so it is for the careerist politician with no ideological goals. Acquiring and maintaining office is the first priority, for socialism cannot be created without one having power. Little consideration is given to the fact that the extent to which one may have to compromise to win office might make it impossible for one to do more than theorize about socialism. However, the leaders of the PNC have been fortunate; they have found themselves in a unique historical context which has allowed them to remain relatively progressive and they have no intention of jeopardizing it by 'tactless adventurism'.

The PPP was partly correct in one suggestion: the human rights posture of the Carter presidency gave rise to a wider acceptance of the idea of ideological pluralism in international affairs and created the perfect environment for the PNC to constitutionalize some of its important socialist goals. But the opportunistic nature of the framework meant that even here it preferred to project these non-ideological universally acceptable provisions such as 'equality of women' and 'land to the tiller'. It is amazing how little attention was given to the fundamental socialist provisions of the 1980 Constitution. It is as if this had been planned by the PNC. Its opponents made much of the provisions dealing with the executive powers which, with a few exceptions which we will consider, are in reality no different from those contained in many other constitutions and which, in the context of Guyanese politics, are largely irrelevant.

It is true that the 1980 Constitution is no more than a piece of paper and that the important socialist principles are only stated as aspirations but the very constitutionalization of these principles could be considered a step forward although it would help if the government adhered to its provisions. In saying this we are quite aware of the contention that the 1980 Constitution might be the *de facto* supreme law but its *de jure* status is somewhat in doubt since it was introduced by a regime which has kept itself in government through electoral fraud.

Important constitutional provisions

The 1980 Constitution did not replace the referendum as a method of changing the constitution but it has different priorities since, according to Dr Shahabbuddeen, it sought to consolidate 'constitutional advance carefully charted and faithfully expressed'. We will begin by considering the provisions which can only be changed by referendum.

Article 164(2:a) enumerates the Articles which can only be changed by referendum (Constitution, 1980). These are Articles 1, 2, 8, 9, 18, 51, 66, 89, 99 and 111. Unlike the old constitution, Article 1 states that

Guyana is a secular, democratic state in transition from capitalism to socialism while Articles 2 and 8 respectively state what should be considered to be the territory of Guyana and that the Constitution is the supreme law. Articles 9 and 18 are also departures from the previous constitution: together they place sovereignty in the hands of the people, to be exercized through the democratic organs established under the constitution and claim that 'Land is for social use and must go to the tiller'. In 1981 a committee under the Agricultural Adviser to the President, himself a large landowner, was set up to 'urgently' advise the Government on the issue. Not much has since been heard of the committee and we are not aware of any significant changes in land policy.

Article 51 describes the Parliament of Guyana as consisting of the President and the National Assembly and Article 66 indicates the conditions under which Parliament may alter the constitution. In Article 89 we find the following: 'There shall be a President of the Co-operative Republic of Guyana, who shall be Head of State, the supreme executive authority, and Commander-in-Chief of the armed forces of the Republic.' Formerly, the President was head of state but not head of government. The new Constitution created an executive President. Articles 99 and 111 elaborate on the executive nature of the Presidency, with Article 111 stating that the President must act 'in accordance with his own deliberate judgement' except in the specific cases where he is required to take advice. A referendum is no longer necessary for changing the provisions dealing with moral justice and the essential freedoms, e.g. those which govern the composition of the National Assembly, the operations of the Elections Commission and the protection of fundamental rights and freedoms. The PNC would be correct in arguing that 'constitutional advance' has made it unnecessary to have to organize a referendum on such issues, for the existence of that obstacle has not prevented it from doing exactly as it pleases! We have stated before that it is in this context that one must analyse the politics of Guyana. Once sufficient weight is given to the fact that it is legitimate and sensible to struggle for the protection of conceptual rights which are violated in practice, the 1980 Constitution is more useful if viewed as an expression of the intentions of the PNC. We cannot agree with those who see it as an elaborate scheme to camouflage the rulers' tyrannical intentions if for no other reason than that the contention has not been adequately demonstrated: neither the internal nor the external position of the party has required a constitution to bolster it either at the time the constitution was introduced or now.

Chapter 2 of the Constitution contains some important pronouncements. Article 13 states that the main objective of the national political system is to extend socialist democracy by providing increasing opportunities for the people to take part in the management of the state, while Article 14 states that the first goal of the economic system 'is the fullest possible satisfaction of the people's growing material, cultural and intellectual requirements, as well as the development of their personality and their socialist relations in society.' Article 15 (2) claims that the national economy will be based on social ownership of the means of production and that it is planned eventually to abolish those conditions which give rise to the exploitation of man by man. It is expected that the economy will develop in accordance with the economic laws of socialism set upon the foundation of socialist relations of production. National economic planning will regulate the state but the widest possible participation of the masses at enterprise, community, regional and national levels is envisaged.

This participation must be based upon co-operativism 'the dynamic principle of social transformation' which shall pervade all relationships in society. Private enterprise is given short shrift in Article 17, which is not surprising since it was roundly condemned in Article 15: 'The existence of privately owned economic enterprises is recognised. Such enterprises must satisfy social needs and operate within the regulatory framework of national policy and the law.' However, a much more vigorous statement defends personal property in the form of dwelling houses and lands, farmsteads, tools, motor vehicles and bank accounts.

Certain rights and duties not contained in the old constitution but consistent with the regime's socialist ideology are also imbedded in Chapter 2. Article 22(1) states that every citizen has the right to work and to be remunerated according to the quality and quantity of such work. Every citizen also has the duty to work. The right to work is guaranteed by an assortment of policy statements such as: 'social ownership of the means of production, distribution and exchange', by socialist planning, development and management, 'by socialist labour laws', and so on. It is difficult to see how these statements could 'guarantee' the right to work in any meaningful way. As the PPP argued, the only real guarantee of the right to work is the existence of employment and, as we have argued below, opportunities for employment have been consistently shrinking in Guyana.

Between Articles 23 and 27 the right to leisure, medical attention and social care in old age, adequate housing and education are all provided for. Article 29(1) states; 'Women and men have equal rights and the same legal status in all spheres of political, economic and social life. All forms of discrimination against women on the basis of their sex are illegal.' Children born out of wedlock are provided with rights equal to those not so born and to discriminate against them is illegal. In this the regime was coming to grips with a situation which many people thought was unjust. Chapter 3 protects the fundamental rights and freedoms of the individual in much the same way as in the old constitution. The right to life, liberty, security of person and the protection of the law is guaranteed to all regardless of race, colour or creed.

In a contribution entitled 'Guyana—The Second Republic' Eusi Kwayana stated his intention to 'show why the rulers decided on a new constitution, and how they plan to use it to keep their class afloat' (*Caribbean Contact*, December 1981, p. 8). It should be noted that here we have a somewhat different argument. The PNC has not used the 1980 Constitution to explicitly, legally entrench itself in government, as was predicted, so Kwayana's contribution now invites us to the search for the rulers' hidden intentions lying under the debris of well-meaning words! This statement by Kwayana provides an interesting focus as we proceed.

Kwayana argued that in drafting the new constitution the hard core of the PNC, aware that it had no popular support, saw itself as a group under seige. Like most ruling classes this hard core equates their class needs with the needs of society, so in their view a threat to them constitutes a threat to the Republic. In the past the regime had used its monopoly over the security forces, the economy, the mass media and various state structures and had exploited racial insecurity to frustrate the legitimate demands of working people. However, with time, the masses found new symbols and began to break out of the oppressive system and the regime panicked.

Kwayana claimed that another key to comprehending the regime's policy is to grasp how they use the term 'national ethos' to justify each new plot against democracy and the deterioration of cultural standards. The concept is used as a blanket justification for the regime's numerous suppressive actions of which the new constitution is only one. 'The second Republic, that is the Constitution, is in fact the ethos of the double dealing, of the fears, the uncertainty, the loneliness, the sense of being besieged, the need to posture, which are such well-known complexes of the core of rulers.' (Ibid.) This may well be true but how does Kwayana go about demonstrating it?

Chapter 5 of the Constitution states that the organs of democratic power in Guyana are the Parliament, the National Congress of Local Democratic Organs, the Supreme Congress of the People, the President and the Cabinet. Parliament consists of the President and the National Assembly. Kwayana considers the power of the President. Article 89 recognizes the President as the supreme executive authority, head of state, and chief of the armed forces. This is not an unusual situation in terms of modern-day presidents but Kwayana argues that: 'The President is not only the supreme executive authority, but the supreme legislative authority, since he has a veto over the acts of the Supreme Parliament and the power to make that veto final.' In a sense this is true but it is taken out of its historical context and so does not put the issue fairly. The President is part of Parliament and without his assent a Bill cannot become law but this is not as serious as it seems when it is realized that where, within a given time, the National Assembly returns a Bill to the President on a second occasion and the latter fails to give assent to it he must dissolve Parliament and call an election. This is not as great a departure from the 1966 Constitution, according to which, if the Prime Minister was defeated in the National Assembly he had the option of resigning and forcing an election.

Kwayana turns to the conditions under which the President could be removed from office. 'The President can only be removed from office when he is least guilty, that is, if he is judged to be insane. But only his own party members of parliament can start the moves to bring this about' (Ibid). This is overstating the case. As will be seen presently, there are other methods for impeaching the President and we need not read anything sinister into the provision that only a member of the

President's party could bring a motion of insanity against him. Firstly, brought by another party it is likely to fail since the President is elected by the majority party in parliament. Secondly, if it is possible for the opposition to win the support of members of the President's party to carry such a motion it should be possible for them to find one member to introduce the issue. Thirdly, the members of the President's Cabinet are responsible to the National Assembly for his actions, and they work more closely with him and are likely to be the first to become aware of and to suffer from his insanity. Finally, many acts of government appear insane to the opposition and if they were able to introduce such a motion they could use it to try to embarrass the government.

When coupled with Article 180, which considers the removal of the President from office for violations of the Constitution or gross misconduct, the restriction that only the President's party can raise the issue of his insanity in the National Assembly is further minimized. The President's insanity would most likely become evident through his misconduct and any member of the Assembly could raise such an issue which, if accepted by one half of its members, begins the process of investigation and possible impeachment. What is much more worrying is that the constitution allows a guilty President to dissolve Parliament and call an election before or after his guilt has been established. It introduces a sort of trial by battle which would be sinister in even the best of electoral systems.

Kwayana rightly mentioned the infamous immunities of the President which allow no redress against a President or ex-President for any acts done during the period of his Presidency. Article 182 states:

1. . . . the holder of the office of President shall not be personally answerable to any court for the performance of the function of his office or for any act done in the performance of those functions and no proceeding, whether criminal or civil, shall be instituted against him in his personal capacity in respect thereof either during his term of office or thereafter.
2. Whilst any person holds or performs the function of the President no criminal proceeding shall be instituted or continued against him in respect of anything done or omitted to be done by him in his private capacity and no civil proceedings shall be instituted or continued in respect of which relief is claimed against him for anything done or omitted to be done in his private capacity.

The ruling party claims that the purpose of providing for a new local government system in the constitution is to entrench and broaden socialist democracy. Kwayana denies this and argues that one reason why it was introduced is that the regime has no mass support and intends to use the new local government system to coerce the masses. For the first time in Guyanese history every area of the country is covered by local government and Kwayana views Article 74(2) as particularly sinister: 'Local democratic organs shall organise popular co-operation in respect to the political, economic, cultural and social life of their areas and shall co-operate with the social organisations of the working people.' He argues that this gives to local authorities the power to force their citizens to co-operate with organizations 'which have no power'. In Guyana, he argues, the doctrine of the supremacy of the party is growing into a doctrine of the monopoly of the party. According to him this point is clearly established by Article 75 which gives local organs the power to take decisions which are binding upon their citizens, agencies, institutions and communities.

In our opinion, it is obvious that other, even more plausible implications, could be drawn from the provisions we have considered. It seems quite clear that the introduction of the new local government system carries more risk for the regime than the benefits Kwayana mentioned would warrant. Perhaps that is why the system has not been implemented as yet. So many tiers of local government would make the manipulation of the numerous elections considerably more difficult and would place a significant number of local councils in the hands of opposition forces which, if Kwayana's argument holds, would also be in a position to use them for their political benefit. The regime did not need to go to these elaborate and risky lengths to organize a radically new system if its chief motivation was to create a legal framework to force the people in the localities to comply with its dictate. It could easily have extended and used the old system. No system of local government could exist without corporate powers; this was as true of the old system as it is of the new.

It is almost impossible to successfully impeach modern Presidents but what are particularly alarming are the President's immunities and the provisions which make it possible for a President, guilty of gross misconduct, to escape all punishment. But, since these provisions do nothing to invalidate the argument that the 1980 Constitution is illegal, they certainly cannot legally protect a PNC President if that party should lose power. Nor do they in any way help to create a more popular legal framework for PNC rule. Given the realities of politics in Guyana, we believe that the 1980 Constitution represents no more than the attempt by a socialist orientated group of people to entrench some of their cherished objectives at the same time as they adopt what they consider to be modern political institutions. This does not mean that such institutional arrangements were not chosen to correspond to the leaders' personal ambitions and with an eye to political advantage.

Contrary to the gloomy predictions that the regime intended to create a one-party state, Article 147 of the constitution states that:

Except with his own consent, no person shall be hindered in the enjoyment of his freedom of assembly and association, that is to say, his right to assemble freely and associate with other persons and in particular to form or belong to political parties or to form or belong to trade unions or other associations for the protection of his interest.

However, the Constitution does include some innovations.

Election of members of the National Assembly is still by secret ballot but the National Assembly now consists of 65 instead of its previous 53 members. The 53 members will continue to be elected in the old way; that is, under proportional representation at general elections. The other 12 members will comprise: one elected by each of the ten Regional Democratic Councils from among their members and 2 representatives of the National Congress of Local Democratic Organs. The earlier designation of Leader of the Opposition has been changed to Minority Leader by Article 110(1). According to the PNC the former title left the impression that the work of the minority in the Assembly was to oppose; while this might be so in developed Western society, the task of such parties in countries like Guyana should be to provide constructive suggestions which will help to foster development.

The National Congress of Local Democratic Organs is another innovation provided for by Article 79 which gives it the responsibility of representing the interests of local government in Guyana. Members of the National Congress are elected by and from the members of the

Regional Councils and such other local councils as may from time to time be prescribed. Since only the Regional Councils are established they each elect two representatives to the National Congress which elects its own Chairman and Deputy Chairman.

The constitution also provides for an institution called the Supreme Congress of the People, consisting of the Members of the National Assembly and the National Congress of Local Democratic Organs. The Congress is essentially a talking shop which makes recommendations to Parliament and the Executive. Only the President has the authority to convene the Congress and since 1981 it has met annually.

6 Central and Local Governments

The Cabinet

Prior to the introduction of the rudiments of cabinet government in 1953, the colony was administered according to the general principles laid down in the 1928 Order in Council which introduced Crown Colony government into British Guiana. Executive authority rested with the Governor and his Executive Council, which was partly elected and partly nominated. The Chief Secretary was responsible for implementing the decisions of the Council through different departments of government. The Office of the Chief Secretary was said to: 'express in administration the will of the Crown as conveyed by the direction of the Governor' (Bacchus, 1967, p. 34).

Each government department was administered by a director: thus, the Department of Agriculture was in the charge of the Director of Agriculture who was responsible for both the professional and administrative aspects of the department's work. The Director was responsible for formulating and implementing policy within the framework set out by the government and some of these heads of Departments were also nominated members of the Executive Council. Department Committees consisted of members of the Legislative Assembly who helped to oversee the work of the departments but they were essentially advisory. The directors had considerable leeway in the formulation and execution of government programmes. Bacchus wrote:

In effect one could say that the different functions of government were, in fact, entrusted to those permanent officers in the Civil Service who could act and in many cases did act without the advice or consent of the popular representatives in the Legislature. This was one of the characteristic features of British Colonial administration in which senior civil servants had political power without political responsibility.' [Ibid.]

The new system which culminated in the 1966 independence Constitution transferred executive authority from the Governor and his Executive Council to the Prime Minister and his Cabinet. The

Governor-General, and after the declaration of a Republic in 1970, the President, acted primarily upon the advice of the Prime Minister who, with his Cabinet, was collectively responsible for the general direction and control of the government. The power to decide who gets what, when and how within the broad framework of government policy was transferred from the departmental Directors to Ministers, and Permanent Secretaries and chief professional officers, e.g. the Chief Education Officer, were introduced to deal, respectively, with the overall administration of the Ministry and the effective conceptualization and implementation of its professional services.

The 1980 Constitution made some significant changes to the relationship between the members of the executive. It created an executive President who is the chief executive authority in Guyana and who is expected to act in accordance with his own judgement, except in situations where he is required to take advice or recommendations from special bodies. The Cabinet is required to aid and advise the President in the general direction and control of the government of Guyana but it is responsible to Parliament for the actions of the executive (Constitution, 1980, Article 106:2). Since the President is an essential element of Parliament this is a most interesting situation.

The Cabinet is made up of the President, the Prime Minister, the Vice-Presidents and such other ministers as may be appointed to it by the President. The President appoints Vice-Presidents, the most senior of whom are the Prime Minister, the Deputy Prime Minister, Senior Ministers, Ministers, Ministers of State and Parliamentary Secretaries, but only the Deputy Prime Ministers and Senior Ministers join the Vice-Presidents as permanent members of the Cabinet. This body is usually chaired by the President and in his absence by the Prime Minister.

The President must appoint his Cabinet from among the members of his party in the National Assembly or from outsiders who are qualified to be elected to the National Assembly. The exception is the Prime Minister who must be an elected member of the National Assembly. Ministers who are non-elected members of the Assembly do not have a vote. It is said that West Indians are perhaps the most governed people in the world, having the highest number of ministers per capita. If that is true for the region, Guyanese are the most governed within the region. After the 1980 election President Burnham appointed 35 Ministers, 10 Regional Chairmen who are responsible for administering the 10 regions of the Country, and who have ministerial status and the Chairman of the National Congress of Local Democratic Organs, who also has senior ministerial rank. In 1980, Jamaica, with more than twice the population, had 14 Ministers and Barbados, 12. At present (1985) in Guyana there are 22 Ministers, not including the 10 Regional Chairmen and the Chairman of the National Congress. By making each Vice-President responsible for a group of Ministries, the vice-presidential system is said to make it easier for the Cabinet to co-ordinate its work and also reduce its membership to a manageable level.

Table 1. Party and Government officials—1985

Name	Government Ministers	Central Executive Committee Members
1. Desmond Hoyte	President: Defence	Leader: Elect*
2. Dr Ptolomy Reid	Special Adviser to President	Deputy Leader (Chairman of CEC): App
3. Hamilton Green	Vice-President & Prime Minister: Production, Agriculture, Public Service, Bauxite & Gold mining	Elect
4. Mohamed Shahabuddeen	Vice-President and Deputy Prime Minister: Attorney-General and Justice	Chairman of the General Council: Elect
5. Ranji Chandisingh	Vice-President and Deputy Prime Minister: National Development	General Secretary: App
6. Viola Burnham	Vice-President & Deputy Prime Minister: Social Infrastructure	Elect
7. Haslyn Parris	Deputy Prime Minister: Economic Planning	Elect
8. Jeffrey Thomas	Senior Minister: Home Affairs	App
9. Robert Corbin	Senior Minister: National Mobilization	Elect
10. Rashleigh Jackson	Senior Minister: Foreign Affairs	App

11. Haroon Raschid	Senior Minister: Energy & Mines	Elect
12. Richard Van West-Charles	Senior Minister Health & Public Welfare	Elect
13. Carl Greenidge	Senior Minister: Finance	—
14. Malcolm Parris	Senior Minister: Education, Social Development and Culture	Elect
15. Donald Ainsworth	Minister: in the Ministry of Education, Social Development & Culture	—
16. Yvonne Benn	Minister: in the Ministry of Education, Social Development & Culture	—
17. Urmia Johnson	Minister: in the Ministry of National Development	Assistant General Secretary: App
18. Dr. Simpson DeSilva	Minister: Agriculture	—
19. Salim Sallahuddin	Minister: Forestry	Elect
20. Roy Fredricks	Minister: Youths and Sports	—
21. Kenneth Denny	Minister: Manpower & Co-operatives	App
22. Searam Prashad	Minister: Transport	Elect
23. Malcolm Corrica	Minister of State: Trade & Consumer Protection	—
24. Harold Singh	Minister of State: Regional Development	—
25. Patrick Denny	—	Executive Secretary: National Orientation & International Affairs: App
26. Oscar Clark	—	Executive Secretary: National Production: App
27. Norma Young	—	Executive Secretary: Personnel Administrative Services: App
28. Golkaran Sharma	—	Executive Secretary: Party Affairs & Mass Organisations: Elect

29. Vincent Britain	—	Executive Secretary: Maintenance & Welfare: App
30. M. Dundas	—	Executive Secretary: Financial Administration & Economic Projects: App
31. James Bovell-Drakes	—	Chairman: Young Socialist Movement: Elect
32. Adam Harris	—	Editor: *New Nation*
33. Robert Willians	—	Elect
34. Hyacinth Godett	—	Treasurer: Elect

*Elect—Elected member.
App—Appointed member.

The Cabinet is serviced by a Cabinet Office, headed by a Secretary to the Cabinet. This office takes its direction from the President, sets out the agenda and provides and circulates the minutes and decisions of the Cabinet. Like the CEC of the party, the Cabinet also has sub-committees consisting of relevant ministers, experts and advisers. Decisions are taken at Cabinet level in much the same way as they are taken in the party system. After the usual discussion, the President sums up, giving his decision and here also important decisions are taken without the knowledge of the Cabinet or even the relevant minister. One is again reminded of Burnham's public announcement of the introduction of free education which is said to have caught the then Minister of Education by surprise.

Local government

As was mentioned in the previous chapter, Article 13 of the 1980 Constitution states that the principal political objective of the state is to extend socialist democracy by providing increasing opportunities for its citizens to participate in the management of their society. Article 12 lays down that: 'Local government by freely elected representatives of the people is an integral part of the democratic organisation of the state.' For decades attempts have been made to create a comprehensive and effective system of local government in Guyana and the PNC has claimed that the system proposed in the 1980 constitution and the Local Democratic Organs Act 1980 provides just such a system, with sufficiently large and well-endowed areas to become viable socio-economic units capable of providing all-round development for their inhabitants. The previous dependency of local upon central government is said to have 'had its inevitable consequence, namely, that Local Government could never develop an independent and self-sustaining life of its own: Central Government kept alive the Local Government system by patronage and largesse.' (Hoyte, 1980). It is claimed that the new local government system will break out of the strangle-hold of the centre and become a vibrant partner in development.

A historical overview of local government in Guyana

We have already discussed the villages established by the Africans immediately upon the abolition of slavery and have pointed to the fact that pressure from the plantocracy led to internal neglect and that while the Africans continued to live in their villages they never provided the basis of a successful peasant economy. As early as 1852, the ruling class were passing laws for the regulation of the villages. Ordinance 1 of that year prohibited the joint purchase of land by more than twenty persons and Ordinance 33 of 1856 stated that where more than ten persons purchased land it must be divided among them and that the individual shares so held would be subject to a monthly rate to provide for the upkeep of the villages. Of course, no rates were levied on the plantations: instead, the public purse was used to aid them in the acquisition of indentured labour. One commentator of the day contended:

While it was desirable to support these services, there was little evidence that smallholders could do so more effectively than a communally held estate; but the prohibition of communalism would divert the ex-slave from large-scale land buying and thus make him more amenable to a return to plantation labour. [Payne, 1978, p. 232].

The municipalities of Georgetown and New Amsterdam were founded in 1782 and 1785 respectively. It was not until 1837 that the citizens of Georgetown were allowed to elect a mayor and town council. To qualify as an elector one had to own property to the value of G$3,200. John Croal was elected as the first Mayor. On 1 September 1891, 106 years after its establishment, the Governor of the Colony, Sir Charles Bruce, conferred a mayor and town council upon New Amsterdam. No other towns were established until 1970 when, as part of a general local government reform programme, Linden, Corriverton and Rose Hall became towns.

In 1907 there was a major local government reform which established Local Government Boards and subdivided the country into four kinds of areas:

1. Urban Sanitary Districts—the municipalities of Georgetown and New Amsterdam;
2. Village Districts—all villages previously declared;
3. County Districts—which had almost similar status as the Village Districts but councillors were nominated by central government;
4. Rural Sanitary Districts—which included all plantations owned by companies and not included in other districts.

In 1931, the establishment of county councils was recommended by the Hector Joseph Committee which also sought the incorporation of sugar estates into the local government system and the appointment of administrative officers and in 1932 District Commissioners were appointed to administer the nine Administrative Districts into which the country was divided. These functionaries exercised wide-ranging powers and reported, through the Chief Secretary, directly to the Governor. They were responsible for all government activities in the district and one of their primary tasks was to supervise the work of the local authorities within their jurisdiction. The District Commissioner system lasted until the coming of the Ministerial system. The Denham Report of 1954 complained that the system of local government was ineffective and in 1955 the Marshall Commission was appointed to 'enquire and report on all aspects of local government in all rural and urban areas in Guiana and to make such recommendations for reforms as may be practicable and desirable.'

Marshall was one of those who believed that local government was central to the operation of a modern democratic state. He argued that properly organized it:

harnesses local enthusiasm; it teaches both electors and elected their civic duties; it trains politicians and officials destined to play important parts in the wider sphere of national government; it avoids bureaucratic government; it gives practice in the use of power; it encourages community mindedness; it avoids the expensive alternative of doing the local work by a series of separate outposts of the central department; and finally it provides the means by which stable local government can continue irrespective of political convulsions at the centre. [Marshall, 1955, p. 15.]

Dr Marshall's main proposals were that Georgetown and New Amsterdam should continue to be municipalities and that there should be a single-tier system of local government. The entire coastland and riverain areas should be divided into eighteen large district councils which would be able to carry out additional responsibilities. Marshall expected the new authorities to undertake many functions then performed by central government and saw the inclusion of the sugar estates into the local government system as a *sine qua non* for the creation of large viable units. The Marshall Report was highly acclaimed and the major criticism levelled against it was that it made unrealistic assumptions about the level of socio-economic development in the rural areas.

With the coming of representative government, demands were increased for improved living standards and the involvement of the people in local affairs. The Colonial Secretary, Lennox Boyd, stated that Marshall's proposals would be implemented but it was not until 1969, when the country had settled down from the political upheavals which resulted from the struggle for independence, that some significant action was taken. In that year the Local Authorities (Elections) Act, the Municipal and District Councils Act and the Valuation for Rating Purposes Act were passed. Boundaries of some villages were extended to include unorganized areas, County Districts were elevated to Village Districts; Georgetown and New Amsterdam were extended and another three towns were created. Local government elections were held in 1970. None had been held since 1959 and none have been held since 1970. In 1973, the Regional system was introduced and Regional Ministers took the place of District Commissioners.

The powers of the new local government system

The regime has argued that the new local government system will not be simply a rate collection agency but will have wide-ranging powers to enable it to stimulate economic development. Among other things, Article 74 of the 1980 constitution states that: 'It shall be the duty of Local Democratic Organs to maintain and protect public property, improve working and living conditions, promote the social and cultural life of the people, raise the level of civic consciousness, preserve law and order, consolidate socialist legality and safeguard the rights of citizens.' Article 6 of the Local Democratic Organs Act 1980 outlines these duties in more specific terms and Article 7 states that, with the approval of the Minister, a local government authority has the power to make regulations for:

1. the proper management and administration of its area;
2. raising revenues by tolls, rates, taxes and dues;
3. the conduct by it of any business which it may be authorized to carry on under its constitutional order;
4. acquiring land compulsorily for local government purposes (Local Democratic Organs Act, 1980).

Article 77 of the Local Democratic Organs Act makes it incumbent upon each region to plan within a national perspective: 'The development programme of each region shall be integrated into the national development plans, and the Government shall allocate funds to each region to enable it to implement its development programme.' Each Region is therefore, required to function as a planning area, to have a planning unit and to co-ordinate, supervise and serve as an information centre for the other sectoral planning areas within it. An important step in making the regions efficient planning, budgeting and development agencies is that which provides for the decentralization of the functions of the treasury and the establishment of sub-treasuries in each region. The annual estimates of each democratic organ in each Region are to be submitted every year to the Chairman of the Regional Democratic Council and he must call a meeting of all the authorities in the Region to discuss the various projects.

The organization of the new local government system

As can be seen in Figure 1, the country is divided into ten Regions and each Region is subdivided into Sub-Regions, Districts, Communities, Neighbourhoods, and People's Co-operative areas, each of which is to have a Council elected on the basis of proportional representation by all those in a given area who are entitled to vote at a general election. At their first meeting, the members of each Council will elect a Chairman and a Vice-Chairman and as a result the party with the majority of elected representatives in the given council will win the Chairmanship and Deputy Chairmanship. The Chairmen and Deputy Chairmen of the Regional Councils and the Mayors and their deputies are full-time officers and the Minister in charge of Regional Affairs is empowered to name other full-time officers of the system.

Each Regional Council sends two of its members as its representatives to the National Congress of Local Democratic Organs and one representative to the National Assembly. The National Congress of Local Democratic Organs is to provide a forum for the co-ordination of local government work, represent the interests of local government in Guyana, investigate and monitor local government operations and perform such other functions as may be prescribed, while representation in the National Assembly is said to give assurance that local government interests are adequately represented in the highest law-making body in the land.

Each local democratic organ has the power to employ such persons as it may need and to set up committees, which may include persons who are not members of the Council, to help them in their work. A Regional Executive Officer, under the guidance of the Regional Chairman, is responsible for supervising the work of the Regional Council and is the accounting officer answerable to Parliament, through the Parliamentary Public Accounts Committee, for all public funds in the Region.

Rating will be undertaken at the Regional and District levels and these two Councils will allocate revenue to the other organs. To facilitate continous co-ordination, two types of organizational relationships are recommended: lateral co-ordination, where the Chairmen of the varying Councils in each Region will arrange regular meetings, and vertical co-operation, where each Council within a Region will elect one of its members to participate, without the right to vote, at meetings of the Council above it. In the case of the city and town councils, a representative participates, without voting rights, at meetings of the Regional Council of the Region in which the city or town is located. However, local government councils which are located in the area of a city or town only possess those functions which are assigned to them by the city or town and do not exercise or perform any other duty conferred by law on similar organs outside the location of the town or city.

As we have stated, elections have only taken place for the Regional Councils but, even in this limited area, in practice, the direct lines of authority and control have given rise to much controversy. For example, the exact position of the National Congress has not been properly established and Regional Chairmen are reluctant to follow its lead. But local government in Guyana cannot be assessed except in the context of the general political struggle taking place in society and the elections to the other tiers of the system could be very embarrassing for the regime. This may well be why they have not yet taken place. Furthermore, even if such elections were held and the system established, its success would depend upon its ability to develop viable economic enterprises. Initially, this would mean that central government must be in a position to provide financing but the present economic crisis in which the country is embroiled does not make that feasible for some considerable time. At best, we could expect the new system to lead to better co-ordination and use of rates, with minimal support from central government, and although this must not be frowned upon, its effect would be very limited. At worst, the present emphasis on trying to decentralize the central departments could lead to greater local bureaucratization and heavier taxes on the local population for limited returns.

State and party relations

Now that we have looked at both party and state structures this is as good a place as any to consider the relationship between the state and the party. When, in July 1972, the Minister of Culture was removed from his position and set to work as an assistant secretary in the party apparatus, one journalist claimed that since the former minister considered the party to be paramount over the Government he should consider his shift to the party as something of a promotion. Thus, for some time before Burnham's statement in the Declaration of Sophia that the party should be geared to claim supremacy over the Government, a youthful and radical wing in the PNC had been claiming that the Government of the day should be obliged to implement the policies of the party which was responsible for its being in power. This position is sufficiently logical to have no need of ideological underpinnings. However, its conceptual base was a mixture of the Leninist concept of the vanguard party and the long debate within the British Labour Party, which has recently been made topical by Tony Benn, that a Labour government should be obliged to implement the policy for which the Labour party had fought at the election. Outlined by the PNC, it was never intended that the party should interfere in the day-to-day workings of government and be above the law. Compared with the relationship which existed then and still exists now between the party and government, it was a progressive concept.

Political leadership in Guyana is charismatic; so far as the mass of people are concerned, the PPP is a personification of Jagan and the PNC was Burnham. The constitution of the PNC restricts the growth of internal party democracy. We have already shown in our discussion of the party that if the leadership is unwilling to relinquish power it would be impossible to remove it. The party can maintain a democratic front only so long as the President and the people he supports remain unchallenged. In discussing the party we have also indicated that since policy is normally pronounced by the Leader after discussion it is quite obvious that party policies cannot go against the wishes of the leadership. Therefore, it is not unreasonable to conclude that the leadership either takes a lead in or must give its support to all major decisions. The people who clamoured for supremacy also supported a system of primaries among party members for those who wanted to hold party office for they realized that it was undemocratic for those who control the state to be beyond the control of the very people they claim to represent most closely.

Their demand for primaries was not taken much notice of by the leadership since, unlike supremacy, which came to mean mere flagwaving—for example, allowing the party's flag to be flown on government buildings—primaries actually threatened people's own positions. The irony is that leftists outside the party, unable to see more than the flagwaving and the inevitable attempts of some minor party members to demonstrate their supremacy in fact, began to attack the doctrine, thus helping to lure these very party members into believing they had power when in fact they had none.

Supremacy of the party remains theoretical, with the leaders using it to infuse a sense of power in the membership. One document argued that the doctrine of supremacy rested upon three main pillars, including the allocation of state funds to the party through the Office of the General Secretary and the Ministry of National Development which uses those funds to hold courses for public servants and mobilize schoolchildren to ensure good attendance at public meetings addressed by Burnham (*Guyana: Fraudulent Revolution*, 1984, pp. 53–8). We have already discussed the motivations behind the establishment of the Ministry of National Development which makes the argument that it was organized to mobilize support by schoolchildren at meetings addressed by Burnham so incomplete as to be a distortion. Furthermore, we have also argued that by the late 1970s this Ministry had become no more than a mobilization machine although, when it was established in 1974, the PNC had been at the height of its popularity and had had no need for this type of mobilization. Indeed, we have already argued that it was the activities of this organization and the ideological and practical proposals which gave rise to it which were responsible for the loss of the party's support base.

Yet another aspect of supremacy is said to be: 'the shifting of the institutional loyalties of the armed forces and the police to the party leaders and away from the titular Head of State' (Ibid.). The African-dominated armed forces had always supported the PNC but the party leaders did attempt to solidify this support. However, there were more fundamental reasons for this and these are outlined in Chapter 9. It is sufficient to say here that they had little to do with the implementation of supremacy. The development and extension of the armed forces is said, in the above-mentioned publication, to be another of the pillars of supremacy. We find this position difficult to accept because it denies that there are legitimate fears about the country's borders. We do not care to argue that the extension of the military is not used to intimidate but again we maintain that the whole point is missed if we fail to put the development in its overall context.

The third and most obvious pillar of supremacy is said to be the regime's control over jobs. In this regard, from the time it took office in 1964, the PNC tended to give first priority to its supporters: we have just made this point in relation to the military. By 1980 the regime was in control of over 80 per cent of the economy and this process not only became more visible but as the Government began to lose support it used this avenue to attempt to force compliance. This process has nothing to do with supremacy and, as has been stated in the chapter on the party, these ordinary party members who came to believe that they had power to question the state elite were the first to be dismissed in the retrenchments which followed the agreements with the IMF.

Supremacy should at least have meant that the Chairmen of the local party structure chosen by the membership of those areas should have been given the opportunity to become the party candidates and Chairmen of the localities, but the party's constitution provides for the opposite. It does not even allow the local membership to freely decide who will be local party leaders. The truth of the matter is that supremacy is a myth maintained by the opposition because, to the uninitiated, it seems a good whip with which to beat the PNC in a country in which only about 1 per cent of the people are party members. On the other hand it is maintained by the leadership to provide the powerless with a sense of power.

After the 1980 election, Burnham appointed a Vice-President for State and Party Relations. Mr Cammie Ramsaroop was also Chairman of the PNC, but he could not work out what exactly the position involved, since, as Table 1 demonstrates, we are not dealing here with a typical communist party in which ministerial and party positions are generally held by different people. In the PNC all the top positions in the state are held by the top people in the party so there can be no great dichotomy as to policy and thus very little need for co-ordination.

7 Mass Organizations and Political Dissent

Mass organizations

Trade unionism

The ruling group in British Guiana had been hostile to the British Guiana Labour Union (BGLU) and had attempted to prevent the union's registration as a legal entity. British capitalism, however, had already come to understand that trade unions were not as threatening as they had first appeared and might even be useful in the modern industrial system, so once the issue of registration reached the Colonial Office it was resolved in the union's favour. The Labour Union was registered in 1921 and it was ten years before another union, the British Guiana Workers' League, was placed on the register.

The influence of the Labour Union far outweighed its size and, although its base was among the urban working-class, branches were established in many villages and a number of plantation workers became members. In 1924, for example, some 4,000 sugar workers, wary of the conditions under which they laboured on the plantations on the East Bank of Demerara, marched to Georgetown to consult with Critchlow; the leaders of this march were said to be members of BGLU. A dozen of them were shot and killed when the colonial authorities tried to disperse the procession. Critchlow and his colleagues believed in the unity of industrial and political action: among other things they fought for rent restrictions and adult suffrage and Critchlow himself eventually became a member of the Government. He also represented the labour movement at international conferences. After a visit to the Soviet Union he voiced his appreciation of what had been done for the working people of that country, only to have the ruling class retort: 'We are very interested in the account Mr. Critchlow brought back to the West Indies of his activities in the Soviet Union. We believe all he has said of his experiences and wish to assure him that if and when it suits him we will accommodate him in a cell.' (Chase, 1965, p. 76).

At the peak of its popularity in 1920, the Labour Union had about 7,000 members but by the time it was registered in 1921 it could only muster 205. Internal divisions had already begun to take their toll; so much so that in 1921 the union was unable to respond effectively to a forced wage reduction. Its initial success in the urban and rural areas left a definite impression that working-class unity had begun but in 1937 the MPCA was formed among the predominantly Indian sugar workers and that unity did not develop. One commentator bemoaned what he considered a lost opportunity and argued that the formation of the MPCA: 'immediately split the solid phalanx of organised workers into two' (Daly, 1970, p. 217). It is questionable whether a solid phalanx had really existed and there was undoubtedly good reason for forming the MPCA. The Labour Union never succeeded in organizing the rural plantation workers on a significant scale and in any event by 1937 it was ineffective and these workers were in need of organization.

In 1941, of the fifteen registered trade unions in British Guiana, four, including the Labour Union, came together and formed the British Guiana Trade Union Council (BGTUC), with the following objectives:

1. To promote the interest of all its affiliated organisations and generally to improve the economic and social conditions of the workers and to secure united action on questions affecting or likely to affect their interests.
2. In furtherance of these objects, the Executive Committee had to endeavour to establish the following measures, and such others as the Council at its Annual Meeting might from time to time approve:
   (i) public ownership and control of natural resources and of services;
   (ii) compulsory acquisition of land by the Government of the Colony for creating peasant proprietorship and land settlement;
   (iii) nationalisation of mines and minerals;
   (iv) nationalisation of public utility services;
   (v) the extension of state and municipal enterprise for the control and provision of social necessities and services;
   (vi) proper provision for the adequate participation of the workers in the control and management of public services and industries. [Chase, 1965, p. 110].

Here again we see unity of political and industrial action but this first attempt to form a radical umbrella organization did not find much support and soon faltered. In 1942 a Labour Department was established to promote the settlement of labour disputes and one of the first acts of the new department was to reorganize a BGTUC shorn of radical objectives. The objectives of the new body were blandly stated to be the promotion of the interests of its affiliates and to improve the economic and social conditions of the workers. However, Jocelyn Hubbard, well-known for his Marxist views, became the Secretary of this new Council so that radical influence was not totally obliterated.

It was Hubbard who represented the TUC at the first conference of the World Federation of Trade Unions (WFTU) which was held in Paris in 1945. In 1949 cold war politics entered the international labour movement when the British, Dutch and North American labour representatives broke away from the WFTU and formed the International Confederation of Free Trade Unions (ICTFU). Given the close ties which existed between British Guiana and Britain, the BGTUC was pressured into withdrawing from the WFTU and joining the ICFTU. The present TUC is still a member of the ICFTU although it has developed working relations with the WFTU.

At the regional level, the TUC is a member of the Caribbean Congress of Labour. In 1926 the first regional labour conference was held in Georgetown, under the auspices of the Labour Union and one of the decisions of that conference was to establish a regional federation of trade unions and labour parties. This proposal, together with others taken at the conference, such as that which called for the creation of a self-governing West Indian Federation, again shows that the delegates saw litle difference between political and labour matters: most leading Caribbean politicians of that generation had begun their careers in the labour movement. It was not until 1943 that a regional labour organization, the Caribbean Labour Congress, came into being but, as happened with the first BGTUC, this organization proved too radical and was disbanded and reorganized in 1945 as the Caribbean Congress of Labour. By the time the PPP took office in 1953, nationally, regionally and internationally acceptable leadership had been found for the trade union movement and this explains why it was necessary for the party to introduce the Labour Relations Bill and attempt to get its own unions recognized if it was ever to succeed in implementing its radical programmes. On the other hand, it also explains why the colonial authorities were determined that the Labour

Relations Bill should not become law. As it turned out, the PPP was thrown out of office and the ensuing split in the party caused a deep rift in the labour movement.

The split in the PPP left the Jagan faction in a dilemma: the Labour Relations Bill was intended to force the sugar industry to recognize the GIWU which was led by Dr Latchmansingh, but now Latchmansingh had thrown in his lot with Burnham. The PPP was forced to form a union to challenge the GIWU and in 1961 the Guiana Sugar Workers Union, which became the GAWU in 1962, came into being and by 1963 it had already overshadowed the GIWU and was challenging the MPCA in the sugar industry. In 1963 the PPP again introduced a Labour Relations Bill which would have forced employers to recognize the union chosen in a poll by the majority of workers. The effect of this would have been to make the GAWU the recognized union in the sugar industry and this time the entire opposition and the TUC, in which the MPCA was a leading force, came out against the Bill. Since the GIWU was dwarfed by the GAWU the PNC had no choice but to support, and seek support from, the MPCA, the very union which Burnham, as Chairman of the 1953 PPP, had wanted to crush. The PNC came to office in 1964 and it took over a decade of struggle and strife in the sugar industry before the GAWU won recognition.

The rules of the reorganized BGTUC made it impossible for radical unions to become members. For example, no union which was affiliated to the WFTU was allowed to become a member. The policy of the new body was highly supportive of the colonial authorities and the trade union movement played a not inconsiderable role in helping to remove the PPP from office. We have already mentioned the excessive number of US 'trade unionists' who entered the country during the later Jagan years. *The Sunday Times* had this to say of the general strike which made a significant contribution to Jagan's downfall:

Jagan was crushed by the longest general strike in history—79 days. Even the mediator sent from London, Robert Willis, then general secretary of the London Typographical Society and a man not noted for his mercy in bargaining with newspaper managements, was shocked.

"It was rapidly clear to me that the strike was wholly political", he said. "Jagan was giving in to everything the strikers wanted, but as soon as he did they erected new demands." [*Sunday Times*, 16 April 1967.]

Part of the opposition's argument was that the strike resulted from the PPP's unwillingness to consult the labour movement so the PNC came to office promising that it would consult with labour on each occasion that its interest was affected by Government's policies. The TUC thereupon transferred the wholehearted support it had given to the colonial authorities to the PNC. In 1970 the Government proposed a Trade Disputes Bill which sought to provide for compulsory arbitration in the event of trade disputes, but it was withdrawn following widespread opposition. In 1975 the GAWU was recognized. In its bid to undermine the PNC the PPP has used this union with devastating effect. Of the 653 strikes which took place in Guyana in 1982 the GAWU called 639 of them! In the early 1970s, while the economy was apparently healthy, the regime paid little attention to the damage which was being done by the GAWU: the control it had over certain key unions and the TUC allowed it more or less to get its own way with the labour movement. Government control of the TUC is made possible by a loophole which gives undue representation to small unions. In his 1983 report to Congress the General Secretary of the TUC noted:

It is illogical that the TUC could be considered as being fully represented when the GAWU with 15,000 members in the sugar industry is not represented on the Executive Council and the Bauxite Unions only partially represented.

It seems illogical also that the present anomalous situation where one union (GAWU) pays affiliation dues to the extent of nearly G$30,000 it is not represented on the Executive Council, while unions with a few hundred members are represented on the Council. [General Secretary's Report, 1984.]

The consistent support which the TUC has given to the regime has not increased the Government's respect for that body. In August 1977, the Executive Members of the TUC and the Government agreed on wage increases for public sector employees for 1977, 1978 and 1979. However, IMF restrictions imposed in 1978 made it impossible for the Government to fulfil the 1979 part of the agreement. Yet, in 1984, the regime passed the Labour (Amendment) Act which gave legal effect to the 1978 agreement and, since the Government did not fulfill the 1979 part of the agreement, the Act also fixed the wages of all public sector employees, whether or not they were covered by the original agreement, at the 1978 level. Wages would now only be increased by agreement between the TUC and the Government.

The immediate cause of the Act was a decision in the Court of Appeal that an employee of the Guyana Sugar Corporation, a state enterprise, was entitled to the increments in salary provided for in his contract of employment. The increments were withdrawn by the corporation when the Government froze wages in 1979. The Appeal Court decision affected hundreds of people and it was estimated that it would cost the industry between G$3 and G$5m. Since public employees are represented by many different unions the Act has the effect of removing the constitutional right of employees to be represented by the union of their choice and since in some cases the government is immune from suit and in others the permission of the Attorney General, himself a member of the government, must be ascertained before proceedings can be begun, if the regime refuses to honour future agreements with the TUC, as it did in the case of the 1978 agreement, there is little the workers or the TUC can do. It must be particularly galling to the TUC that at no stage was it consulted about the Bill.

The Act came into being at a time when the regime was under heavy pressure to significantly increase the wages of public service employees. By making the TUC, which it controlled, the bargaining agent for the workers, the Government had hoped to bypass the vigilance of the individual unions. As we have seen before, an ironic streak seems to run through Guyanese history: little was the PNC to know that by the end of 1984 it would have lost control of the TUC! The process which led to its defeat began with its application for an IMF loan in 1978. By 1979 the strictures of the IMF had begun to bite and workers in the urban bauxite towns and the commercial areas of Georgetown, the traditional support base of the PNC, began to take industrial action which eventually led to an alliance between four unions which had for years been against the regime: the National Association of Agricultural, Commercial and Industrial Employees (NAACIE), the University of Guyana Staff Association (UGSA), the Clerical and Commercial Workers' Union (CCWU) and, of course, the GAWU.

Table 2. Membership of the TUC—1984

Unions	Membership
Pro-government unions	
1. Guyana Labour Union	4,000
2. Guyana Workers' Union	2,500
3. Amalgamated Transport and General Workers' Union	3,000
4. Association of Masters and Mistresses	300
5. Union of Agriculture and Allied Workers	2,000
6. Guyana Co-operative Mortgage Finance Bank Staff Association	450
7. National Union of Public Service Employees	2,500
8. Postal and Telecommunications Workers' Union	2,500
9. Printing Industry and Allied Workers' Union	1,100
10. Guyana Local Government Officers' Association	800
11. Guyana National Co-operative Bank Staff Association	800
12. Manpower Citizens' Association	1,000
13. Guyana Teachers' Union	8,000
14. Guyana Field Foremen and Supervisors' Union	1,700
15. Public Employees' Union	600
16. Sawmill and Forest Workers' Union	1,000
17. Government Employees' Union	2,000
'Pro-labour' unions	
1. Guyana Agriculture Workers' Union	15,000
2. University of Guyana Staff Association	600
3. Public Service Union	9,000
4. Guyana Mine Workers' Union	5,000
5. Clerical and Commercial Workers' Union	3,000
6. National Association of Agricultural, Commercial and Industrial Employees	900
7. Guyana Bauxite Supervisors' Association	850

Between 1979 and 1984 the number of these 'pro-labour' unions was increased by the two bauxite unions: the Guyana Mine Workers' Union (GMWU) and the Guyana Bauxite Supervisors' Union (GBSU). The economy of the bauxite industry had reached such a state by the first years of the 1980s that the regime was forced to dismiss thousands of workers and cut the working week from five to three days. This situation, together with the heightened political agitation of the WPA, led by Walter Rodney, forced the unions to better represent their members and this meant confrontation with the PNC. This group was joined in 1984 by the Guyana Public Service Union (PSU). When the PNC lost the support of this union it must have felt as if the roof had caved in for the public service unions had been instrumental in the movement which had brought down the PPP. Public servants had been some of those hardest hit by the IMF decision to curb the public sector and they had had to face retrenchment, redeployment and every other terminology that the regime coined to conceal the large-scale dismissals which were taking place. Those who still had jobs had their wages frozen at the same time as prices rocketed. The urban consumer price index rose from 100 in 1970 to 196.5 in 1978 and it was 448.5 in 1983. The PSU was therefore compelled by these conditions to turn against the PNC and although its President (and President of the TUC) George Daniels continues to claim that he is not anti-PNC he has been steadily driven into confrontation with the regime.

To its dismay, the PNC looked on as the pro-labour faction won 13 of the 26 seats on the Executive Council of the TUC at the 1984 Congress and when one considers the key positions the faction controls it is clear that it is dominant. The regime is now doing all it can to remove Daniels from his position as President of the PSU—and hopefully also from the presidency of the TUC—and to regain the control it has lost.

The Women's Movement

Perhaps the closest the Women's Movement came to being a mass movement, both in the sense of representing the objective interest of the masses of women and of involving a large cross-section of them in the struggle to improve their socio-economic position was in the period immediately preceding the split in the national movement. For some considerable time before that women's groups were to be found in religious and charitable organizations but in 1946 the first conscious attempt was made to organize women politically with the formation of the Women's Political and Economic Organization (WPEO). Janet Jagan was its President and Winifred Gaskin, later to become a PNC minister and ambassador, became its Honorary Secretary. The WPEO supported the call for universal adult suffrage and its members took an active part in demonstrations against the colonial administration. However, even if the organization can be said to have represented the real interests of women in Guyana, its membership base was weak and the vast majority of women were unaware of its activities. By 1948 the WPEO had collapsed and it was not until 1953, with the formation of the Women's Progressive Organization (WPO), the women's arm of the PPP, that an organization was created which caught the imagination of a large number of women.

Among the leaders of the WPO were Janet Jagan, Jessica Huntley and Jane Philips-Gay. The WPO fought with the PPP in the period leading up to the 1953 general election but the split which divided the party had a similar effect upon the organization. Jane Philips-Gay became Chairman of the PNC's Women's Auxiliary and Janet Jagan stayed with the WPO. Since the 1955 split of the WPO there has been no broad-based women's organization able to span the racial barrier. The WPO and Women's Auxiliary were most active in the period 1957 to 1964 as they became locked in the battle to maintain or remove the PPP from office.

In recent years, however, women of all races have become increasingly conscious that they have special interests which make it necessary for them to give support to women's programmes although they may not be part of an organization. The regime has tried to deal with these aspirations although the PNC cannot claim to have mass support among women. We have already seen that the membership of its own women's arm was only 825 in 1983 and women are being particularly affected by recent government policy which has made the acquisition of adequate food for old and young alike very difficult. Of course, this does not mean that the WRSM, the WPO and other groups and institutions which cater for women are not useful. On the contrary, they articulate and formulate programmes which are of particular importance to women and either help to implement them or criticise and pressure the regime to do so.

In 1972 the Council on the Affairs and Status of Women in Guyana (CASWIG) came into being as an advisory body in the Ministry of Labour. Its objective is to secure greater participation by women in all areas of Guyanese society. It conducts investigations into the working conditions of women and makes recommendations to the Ministry. CASWIG organizes consumer education and child care programmes and attempts to find employment for women. It works through the different women's organizations such as the Guyana Federation of Women's Institutes and the Young Women's Christian Association. In 1980 its constitution was altered and its name changed to the Conference on the Affairs and Status of Women in Guyana to facilitate greater participation by the various organizations in its work.

In 1980 CASWIG and the WRSM proposed to the Cabinet that national governmental machinery be established to co-ordinate the activities of women in Guyana. The proposals were accepted and the Women's Affairs Bureau was established in January 1981 having as its Director a minister of the Government. The new body is expected to work closely with non-governmental organizations to promote the interests of women. The functions of the Bureau are:

1. To provide general co-ordinating services for co-ordinating developmental programmes for women in Guyana.
2. To impact on policies and programmes of relevant Ministries to ensure that their programmes are designed to cater for the needs of women.
3. To support the establishment and development of Women's organisations, especially those whose objectives are in conformity with the stated objectives of the UN Decade for Women.
4. To give technical and other assistance to projects and activities which contribute to the economic, political, social and cultural advancement of women.
5. To assist the relevant organisations and agencies in designing and organising training courses to impart and upgrade skills of women and to enable them to fill positions at all levels in established agencies of all types, as well as organise them for self-employment.
6. To liaise with governmental and non-governmental agencies and promote functional co-ordination for accelerated progress in the areas of employment, health and nutrition, education, legislative measures and social welfare which are identified in the World Plan of Action for women.
7. To ensure that general educational objectives and curricula support the development strategies aimed at enhancing women's participation in political, economic and social development.

8. To initiate research and embark on the collection of statistical data in an effort to obtain information on the participation of women in areas such as educational institutions and in various sectors of the labour force.

9. To initiate research, and embark on the collection of statistical data and other information for planning and training purposes and to facilitate and determine action for resolving problems.

10. To collaborate with the mass media personnel in promoting programmes, publications, songs, plays, etc., for the eradication of the derogatory allusions and unflattering images connected with women.

11. To foster and maintain contacts, and exhange information, plans and ideas with national and international organisations and agencies concerned with the Affairs of Women.

12. To collaborate with international agencies and institutions which have relevant objectives for Guyana's thrust in an effort to secure financing for projects for groups of women who will be involved in income generating programmes. [*Women's Affairs Bureau*, 1982, pp. 5–6.]

The Women's Affairs Bureau has been involved in the co-ordination of many important projects with respect to the rights of women. For example, it helped with the work of a committee which was appointed to recommend necessary amendments to Guyanese law to give effect to the constitutional provisions which provide for the equality of women. The committee was chaired by Desiree Bernard, a judge of the Supreme Court, and it made thirty-five recommendations, many of which had been implemented by the end of 1984. It recommended changes in the laws relating to maintenance and affiliation; equalizing rights relating to the acquisition and division of property; giving equal rights to children born out of wedlock, equalizing the pension rights of men and women, etc.

Regional and international contacts are maintained with other women's groups and organizations likely to assist the women of Guyana. In 1972 a Women's Desk was established at the Caribbean Community Secretariat in Georgetown and the movement works closely with it and with the Caribbean Women's Association. In July 1980 Guyana signed the Convention for Elimination of all Forms of Discrimination Against Women and the Women's Affairs Bureau is co-ordinating and monitoring the implementation of the Convention in Guyana.

Table 3. Percentage of males and
females in employment

	Males	Females
1970	81.1	18.9
1977	73.4	26.6
1980*	70.0	30.0

* Projected
Source: Report on Guyana, 1980.

There are no great institutional obstacles to women attaining equal rights with men in Guyana. Slavery and indentureship threw the majority of women side by side with men in the collective struggle for survival. But most men still hold the belief that the place of women is in the home and that even if women are not inferior they need the physical and moral protection of men. However, Table 3 shows that, even with the drastic recession in the economy, when compared with men, more and more women have been joining the labour force. Primary education is compulsory in Guyana for both sexes and although there is still some bias against educating women, mainly in the rural areas, it is steadily decreasing. It is significant that women students now dominate some of the areas once considered the preserve of men. In 1980 70 per cent of the classes in bricklaying and plumbing consisted of women and increasing numbers of them are training and finding employment in carpentry, welding and other traditionally male occupations. Between 1975 and 1979 the percentage of women graduating from the University of Guyana rose from 24 to 36 (Report on Guyana, 1980).

The regime has tried to redress the balance between men and women but a weak economy and rising unemployment are serious obstacles in the path of progress. Furthermore, the political divide means that while many of the changes are helpful to women, the vast majority of women are not part of the process which makes such changes possible. For better or worse, the changes are handed down. Indeed, when one looks carefully at the leadership and regular following of the different government-sponsored organizations, one finds essentially the same small group of women—who are supportive of the

PNC—in control. As we have seen, Burnham's widow heads the WRSM, the Women's Affairs Bureau is led by a minister of the government, and CASWIG by a parliamentary secretary in the PNC Government.

Political dissent

Political dissent does not express itself in Guyana as it does in the communist world since, unlike most communist countries, political groups and parties have a constitutional right to exist in Guyana. The problem for the Government, which does not intend to lose office, is how to contain the activities of such groups within manageable limits and the design of opposition groups is to break out of these constraints to create conditions which will lead to the destruction of the regime. The argument then is not about the right to dissent but is concerned with the numerous violations of those rights by the regime.

Not a day passes without those in opposition to the Government making some claim that their human rights have been violated by the regime. At the time of writing, an issue of the PPP's *Mirror* carried the caption 'Thugs Break up Meeting' and went on to claim that, in the presence of policemen who turned a blind eye, PNC elements broke up a public meeting which was being held by the PPP (*Mirror*, 3 February, 1985). Another article a few days later claimed that the PNC had broken up a meeting of the Guyana Council of Churches which was called to discuss the deteriorating economic situation.

A most fundamental violation of political rights occurs when a government takes steps to perpetuate itself in office, contrary to the constitutional rights of the people. We have already stated that sufficient evidence exists from a wide variety of sources to leave one in no doubt that the electoral process is subverted by the ruling party and even the United States State Department which did so much to put the PNC in power has felt obliged to document other areas of abuse:

By law, all citizens are eligible to participate in the political process, and citizenship may not be denied on political grounds. In fact, participation in opposition political groups has led to reprisals by the Government. These reprisals have included dismissals from employment, interruption of supplies to businessmen, attacks in the offical press, police harassment, transfers to remote sections of the country, and denial of earned promotions and benefits.

Available information indicates that the Government was implicated in the 13 June death of WPA activist Walter Rodney and in the subsequent removal of key witnesses from the country. [*Human Rights Violations in Guyana*, 1982, p. 4.]

The most serious violations of human rights are liquidations and tortures and it is sometimes claimed that compared with Third World standards the PNC regime is saintly. We think it best to point out that no one aspires to this barbarous so-called Third World behaviour and that the same cannot be said when the regime is compared with the political standards of the Commonwealth Caribbean.

The tactic of the Government, even concerning killings in which it may not have been involved, is to refuse to carry out the necessary public inquiry. In 1973, a lecturer at the University of Guyana and a well-known opponent of the regime was shot and seriously injured in what many people believed to have been an attempted assassination, but nothing further was heard of the incident. In 1976 PPP Executive Committee member Isahak Basir was shot and seriously wounded by police on the Essequibo without anything further being heard of the matter. In 1979 WPA activist Ohena Koama was shot and killed in Georgetown by police who claimed that he was carrying arms, but no inquest was held. Again, in October 1979, a Government minister, Vincent Teekah, was shot and killed; Burnham swore revenge but no inquest was held. But perhaps the death most Guyanese and Caribbean people will remember is that of the internationally respected historian and WPA activist, Walter Rodney, which occurred in 1980.

The United States State Department believed that the Government of Guyana was implicated in the death of Rodney, who was killed when a small transmitter which was in his possession blew up in the vicinity of the Georgetown prison. On the face of it, the regime had good reason for wanting Rodney out of the way. Having built himself an international reputation as an academic and revolutionary activist he returned to Guyana where the regime refused to allow him to take up a position at the University of Guyana which had been previously promised him. For his part, Rodney used the extra time this afforded him to agitate on behalf of the WPA, which began to erode the PNC's urban support. If the equation outlined in Chapter 2 has any validity it is clear that Rodney was becoming a threat to both the PNC and to international capital. As a Marxist, if he was allowed to make revolution, international capital would have been in the same position as it was prior to the overthrow of the PPP. What Jagan was in terms of electoral politics in the 1950s and 1960s Rodney became in terms of revolutionary politics in the 1980s. In 1964, Jagan committed to the electoral process, was removed by electoral manipulation: in 1980, Rodney , committed to revolution, could only be removed by violence.

The WPA continues to claim that Rodney was assassinated by the regime which had placed a bomb in the transmitter which he had received from a sergeant in the Guyana Defence Force and was about to test. The regime claimed that Rodney intended to use the bomb to break into the prison and release the inmates in a sensational propaganda coup. There is a third point of view which contends that the regime was losing a significant amount of equipment from the army and suspected that it was getting into the hands of the WPA. In order to teach the WPA that such acts could be costly, the regime arranged for the party to be given a bomb instead of the transmitter it required. According to this theory, it was only by chance that Rodney collected the transmitter and was killed. Be that as it may, the truth is not yet known, for once again there has been no public inquest into the death. By not allowing public inquiries into these incidents the PNC may well be attempting to cover up its involvement in some of them but there is a more subtble implication which should not go un-remarked. When enquiries are not held, the perpetrators of crimes are allowed to run free and public memory is short. The impression is thus left that no one really cares and so it is not sensible to risk one's life in confronting the regime.

The Government's total monopoly of the mass media deserves some attention. Mainly through nationalization, between 1973 and 1976, the Government gained control of 90 per cent of the mass media. In 1973 it took the *Guyana Graphic* from an irate Lord Thompson and it became the *Chronicle* in 1976. There are no evening papers and the *Chronicle* is the only national daily. The PPP *Mirror* and the *Catholic Standard*, a weekly published by the Catholic Church, are kept on a tight rein by the regime which controls the distribution of newsprint. In 1979, Radio

Demerara, a subsidiary of Rediffusion, was acquired by the state and merged with the Guyana Broadcasting Corporation, as its second channel.

In the early 1970s a communication theory called 'development support communications' was said to underline the operation of this state monopoly. In a nutshell, at the core of this theory was the idea that the media should be used to transmit information supportive of the development programmes of the Government. It is obvious that in reality such an outlook would effectively close the doors of these institutions to the opposition since all criticism could be construed as destructive of national development goals. In 1980, the US State Department reported that:

Although the Constitution guarantees freedom of speech, press, religion and assembly, the past two years have witnessed a significant curtailment of those rights by the government. The daily press and local radio are government-owned and serve as organs of the ruling party. The only private radio station was purchased by the government in 1979. [Ibid., p. 19.]

8   The Guyanese Economy

Both the Government and the official opposition in Guyana agree that the Co-operative Republic is in deep crisis and there is also general agreement as to its immediate cause. In presenting the 1984 budget, the Minister of Finance and Economic Planning repeated the generally accepted explanation: 'The production sector of Guyana', he stated, 'has undergone a marked decline over the last three years. This decline reflects in part the global depression. It does in addition also point to the cumulative and deleterious impact of the post-1980 production crisis' (Budget, 1984, p. 33).

As will be seen below, however, the production crisis began long before 1980. Where Government and opposition disagree is over their explanations for the economic collapse. The Government's reasoning comes primarily in market, technical and managerial terms, while other commentators postulate an underlying political crisis. In 1982, Professor Clive Thomas of the University of Guyana wrote:

At this juncture, the crisis of production is totally political, as the political form and nature of the state becomes the primary constraint to regenerated production. The state in its own self-interest denies this and through its control of the media seeks also, to deny the assistance of any such reality. It is out of this process, however, that widespread acceptance grows to the notion that a 'political solution' has to precede the implementation of an economic one. [Thomas, 1982, p. 58.]

Most Guyanese believed that, given their country's many natural resources the achievement of political independence could only have been the prelude to the more attractive goal of economic independence. However, this was not to be. In the two decades that have since elapsed, Guyana has remained tied to the same productive activities which had underlain its colonial status and although independence has brought new forms of organization, the basic economic structure has remained largely the same. Some of the blame may be placed upon imperialism and the international economic system within which the country operates, but for reasons which are outlined throughout this volume, this has also been a conscious choice on the part of the leadership of the PNC. Guyana's major failing has been its inability to expand its productive capacity, both in terms of the diversification of its economy and in increasing the production of its traditional resource base. As a result, the country has failed to break out of the vicious circle of economic weakness and poverty which it has been bequeathed.

The colonial economy

British Guiana exhibited all the typical characteristics of underdevelopment inherent in colonial status. Its economy was dominated by the production of three primary products: sugar and bauxite for international markets and rice which was, and still is, the population's basic staple, but also affords export surpluses. With the exception of rice, the main productive activities were controlled by foreign companies which consequently had a profound influence upon the political and economic life of the colony. Financially, commercially and technologically, the umbilical cord which so firmly secured British Guiana to the economic influences of the outside world resulted in a continuous and substantial overseas drain of the nation's wealth, with a limited multiplier effect being generated within the colony itself. Economic activity was so constrained within this narrow specialization, however, that the colony was dependent upon external sources for a wide range of products vital to its progress. In addition to petroleum (the main source of power), fertilizers and other agricultural chemicals, machinery spare parts and components, reliance on a range of foodstuffs and other consumer goods occasioned much 'unnecessary' dependence on overseas suppliers, particularly in the light of the colony's agricultural base. Indeed, apart from rice and sugar cultivation, and cattle ranching on the Rupununi uplands in the south-west, domestic agriculture was limited to small-scale vegetable and fruit growing, while many families supported a small allotment and an animal or two.

Although the incidence of economic activity fluctuated both over the short and the long term, there existed a permanent reservoir of labour, surplus to productive requirements, which in the years between the Second World War and independence averaged around 25 per cent of the total labour force. The economy was therefore unable to support a sufficient level of employment and consequently a significant number of the people lived at very low levels of subsistence and were in turn a continual burden on productive capacity. Further, given the inadequate resource base, many of the remainder experienced conditions of underemployment, either working seasonally or for only a few hours every day or even week, or simply working inefficiently due to an insufficiency of adequate equipment. British Guiana, then, was for the most part in a general state of economic underdevelopment with a poor infrastructure, a paucity of productive capital, inadequate economic and social services and a level of per capita income (1950–56 averaged G$350 per annum) which gave the majority of the population a living standard barely above subsistence. The economic system simply functioned for the exploitation of a few products which were in demand on the overseas market. Everything else was completely ancilliary to this and although some spin-offs were experienced they were minimal and the main benefits of sugar growing, or bauxite mining were as apparent in London or New York as they were to the population of Georgetown. What did emerge was an enclave society, a small minority, which satisfied its wants, not through the consumption of goods produced within British Guiana, but as a result of imports from overseas. It is the main contention of this chapter that in the two decades that have elapsed since independence little has really changed, and herein lies the central weakness of the Guyanese economy.

Like most of its neighbours, colonial Guiana was geared to the production and export of cane sugar and most of the estates were controlled by overseas, mainly British, interests. By the end of the nineteenth century, limited liability companies had become the dominant form of ownership within the sector and by the time the industry was nationalized in 1975–6 two companies (particularly Booker-McConnell, which established an early dominance upon which it was to build a world-wide reputation) controlled 90 per cent of the productive capacity and owned all the eleven sugar mills which then existed. Although sugar cultivation often fluctuated in the short run owing to weather, labour unrest, culture disease and other adverse conditions, the long-run trend of output was upward. By 1960 the annual output of cane had reached 334,000 tons and although in the early 1960s it declined as a result of internal unrest, it had recovered to 309,000 tons by 1965.

Although rice was cultivated during the period of slavery, it was almost entirely organized on small-scale, subsistence lines until the late nineteenth century when ex-indentured Indian workers, experienced in paddy cultivation, began to appreciate its commercial potential. Rice growing had traditionally taken place on small parcels of land leased from the sugar estates or from the few rich landowning families, but commercialization brought consolidation of land units for the enjoyment of economies of a larger scale of cultivation. By 1914 British Guiana was beginning to establish its reputation as the rice bowl of the Caribbean, with a growing export surplus. This position deteriorated between the two World Wars, but after years of instability, rice production recovered and by the mid-1950s annual output stood at 70,000 tons and there were over 25,000 people growing and harvesting the crop. Despite the general neglect of their responsibilities by the landowners, the industry saw, over the next decade, a significant expansion and on the eve of independence 35,000 people farmed 266,000 acres, an increase of nearly 70 per cent on the 1957 acreage and annual production increased to 164,000 tons. This saw a major boom in exports and in 1962 they stood at over 90,000 tons, with around one-third of this going to Cuba.

The third major component of British Guiana's economy, bauxite mining, was the most recent to develop and the industry did not really begin until the 1920s, when bauxite became prized by the industrial countries as the base ore in aluminium smelting and for the manufacture of refractory products. The main deposits of bauxite are found between the Berbice and Demerara rivers, at Linden and eighty miles further east at Kwakwani. Because of the high capital cost of initial developments, the industry was owned and controlled from the start by overseas interests, with Alcan operating around 80 per cent of capacity at Linden and Reynolds directing the more limited operations at Kwakwani. Despite its relatively recent origins, bauxite mining had, by the 1950s, become a significant productive sector, stimulated first by the considerable war demand and then by the massive consumer durable boom in North America and Europe. By the mid-1960s the mining of bauxite comprised over 10 per cent of the colony's GNP and contributed a quarter of total export value (*Bank of Guyana Report*, 1969). Apart from bauxite mining, the only other significant economic activities in the interior were cattle ranching on the Rupununi plains, forestry and the sporadic mining of gold and diamonds.

Paradoxically, given the wealth of natural resources, land hunger was a persistent problem. The major agricultural activities of rice and sugar growing were tied to the coastal plains which, owing to inadequate capital expenditure, were forced to maintain a precarious balance between excessive and inadequate irrigation. Thus, with over 90 per cent of the total land area forming the interior and largely beyond the limits of viable usage and with the failure to fully exploit the coastal plain itself, Guyana's resource base has for long failed to achieve its true potential.

Although, for most people, the colony managed to sustain a minimal level of economic growth and by the post-war years, along with Barbados, Jamaica and Trinidad and Tobago, dominated the economics of the Commonwealth Caribbean, because of its dependence upon world market prices, this position was never stable. This, together with the drain of resources overseas owing to foreign ownership of the major sources of economic activity, led to a weak multiplier effect which resulted in productive potential being maintained at a consistently low level. British Guiana failed, indeed did not really attempt, either to develop productive activities to satisfy the indigenous population's needs, or to broaden its export base. Neither did it improve the infrastructure much beyond the narrow needs of the export sector and even then its commitment was distinctly atrophied. The result, then, was an economic system which failed to provide the necessary requirements and an adequate basis for the dramatic political changes which lay ahead.

The advent of political independence in 1966 was not paralleled, not immediately at least, by a commensurate change in the economic system. Although the Government proceeded to open up the economy still further to external influences, with the introduction of a number of monetary and fiscal incentives to maximize foreign involvement, so-called 'industrialization by invitation', there were few changes in real terms, and economic activity was seemingly to rely on the same productive activities, organized in very much the same way as in colonial days. The year 1966 saw the introduction of a development plan drawn up by Professor Arthur Lewis which was based upon Puerto Rico's economic strategy. Guyana, however, did not have the same access to the United States market, neither did it have the same attractive investment opportunities and the plan was finally abandoned in 1969 after proving totally inappropriate. In its wake, the plan left a weak, confused and little-changed industrial sector and agricultural activities which were neglected after years of growth.

Growth and decline

In 1970 a sharp change of policy took place when Guyana declared itself a Co-operative Republic. A policy of co-operative self-reliance was now proclaimed. According to official sources this meant: 'that Guyana must itself produce the basic requirements of its people, must itself decide on its trade and other external policies' (King, 1973, p. 3). In keeping with its concept of self-reliance, from about 1970, the Government of Guyana began to seek meaningful participation in the management of the multinational companies which operated within its boundaries. 'The achievement of economic independence', it was argued, 'is yet another goal of our society. The necessity therefore arises for changes in the ownership structure of the economy without which the process of economic development would be meaningless' (Ibid., p. 4).

Disagreement over the terms of participation led to a pattern of nationalization which by 1980 left the regime in control of over 80 per cent of the economy. In 1971 and 1975 respectively, the Government nationalized the Demerara Bauxite Company Ltd, a subsidiary of the Aluminium Company of Canada (ALCAN), and Reynolds (Guyana) Mines, a subsidiary of Reynolds Metals of the United States. In 1975 and 1976 it took over the assets of the two British multinationals, Jessel Securities Ltd and Booker McConnell Ltd which controlled the sugar industry. In this process of nationalization the state took over some thirty-two companies involved in activities ranging from sugar growing and processing to manufacturing, commerce and communications. In addition, over a dozen new companies were established under the umbrella of the Guyana State Corporation (GUYSTAC).

The pattern of nationalization adopted by the Government has been described as the 'mortgage finance type' (Kwayana, 1976), the basic feature of which was said to be the over-generous compensation payments which made domestic assets a burden on future foreign exchange earnings since compensations were to be paid out of such earnings. Furthermore, it is said that some contracts of purchase left the multinationals with obligations to provide services in relation to technology, management, marketing and the purchase of equipment. Indications that the Government might have been too generous are deduced from the fact that not a single multinational has publicly quarrelled with the terms of the take-over and a few, because of their own financial difficulties, may have even offered to sell their property to the regime (ibid.).

While it is true that the Government paid something in the region of G$800m. for the nationalized assets, the above argument lacks realism. In the first place, could the Government have afforded not to pay? Geopolitical realities would indicate not. In the early 1960s, the PPP had been manoeuvred from office by the United States and British Governments simply for making overt socialist noises (Jagan, 1966) and we now have the examples of Chile under Salvador Allende, Jamaica under Michael Manley, Grenada under the People's Revolutionary Government of Maurice Bishop and the present Nicaraguan situation as indicators that non-payment would have been foolhardly indeed. Furthermore, the fact that the parties to the negotiation have made no public statement of dissatisfaction could be taken as proof of their 'success', and not as proof of the subjugation of one party by the other. In any case, to offer unacceptable conditions would have been to court the same results as not to pay. As to the other aspects of the contract dealing with the provision of services by the multinationals, there is no proof that these were foisted on the regime and were not necessary for the effective operation of the enterprises. But although opponents of the PNC make much political capital out of the nationalization payments, by 1984 it only amounted to 4 per cent of total external debt (Budget, 1985, p. 52).

Although, in the first few years of the 1970s, the economy was precariously poised, advantageous prices for Guyana's three major exports: sugar, rice, and bauxite, picked up in 1974 and made possible a real increase in export receipts of about 124.2 per cent when 1975 is compared with 1970 (Table 4). Imports also increased by 109.2 per cent but although most of the indicators doubled or trebled between 1970 and 1975, as Table 4 demonstrates, inflation was already taking its toll. The GDP of 1975 was 2.3 times above that of 1970 but that was a mere 62.5 per cent increase in real terms. The increase in export prices also disguised the increasing cost of vital imports. In particular, oil imports

Table 4. Total and percentage change of selected indicators

G$m. Indicators	1970 Totals	1975 Totals	real % change over /70	1983 Totals	real % change over /70	real % change over /75
GDP at factor cost	467.0	1,096.4	62.5	1,200.0	−42.0	−64.7
GNP at market prices	490.5	1,139.1	60.7	1,296.0	−41.1	−63.3
Total investments (public and private)	123.2	320.0	79.8	395.0	−28.5	−60.2
Total consumption (public and private	414.7	845.3	41.1	1,310.0	−29.6	−50.1
Total private consumption	327.9	598.7	26.4	822.0	−44.1	−55.8
Exports	264.8	858.0	124.2	580.0	−51.2	−78.2
Imports	268.2	810.6	109.2	745.0	−38.1	−70.4
Public debt	267.2	932.6	141.5	5,928.4	394.7	104.8
Security	17.4	44.5	77.0	126.1	61.6	−8.7
Health	11.0	22.7	42.8	46.9	−4.9	−33.4
Education	19.1	44.6	61.6	97.5	13.8	−29.6

Source: Bank of Guyana Statistics, 1985; calculated from the inflation rates in Table 5

increased in value from G$23.0m. in 1970 to G$430.7m. in 1981, while the imports of all capital goods, mainly plant and machinery, increased from G$96.6m. to G$303.0m. between 1970 and 1976. Invisible imports made the position even bleaker as they increased from G$69.3m. in 1972 to G$398.0m. in 1983. Many of these increases were due to increasing import volumes but price inflation was evident.

Table 5. Guyana Urban
Consumer Price Index
1970–100

Period	All Items Index
1970	100.0
1971	101.0
1972	106.0
1973	114.0
1974	133.9
1975	144.5
1976	157.5
1977	170.5
1978	196.5
1979	231.4
1980	264.0
1981	322.7
1982	390.2
1983	448.5

Source: Bank of Guyana, 1985

The favourable export prices of the first half of the 1970s waned in the second half at the same time as inflation accelerated. But, as Table 6 shows, the dependence upon external sources for vital inputs, especially petroleum, which during the period regularly comprised over 40 per cent of total visible import value, contributed a great deal to the deterioriation of the balance of trade. In real terms, the 1983 GDP was 42.7 per cent below that of 1970 and some 64.7 per cent below 1975. Resources which went into private consumption decreased 44.1 per cent and 55.8 per cent respectively when comparison is made of the years 1970/83 and 1975/83. The decrease in consumer imports was due to the introduction of the self-reliance strategy which focused upon import substitution and which itself grew out of a shortage of foreign exchange.

Table 6. Unit value of major exports
(G$ per long ton)

Year	Sugar	Rice	Calcined Bauxite
1970	261.2	309.9	68.8
1971	273.6	818.8	81.1
1972	339.3	360.7	100.1
1973	337.0	520.8	114.6
1974	941.7	960.7	164.0
1975	1,449.4	1,034.1	211.3
1976	871.0	1,036.6	260.7
1977	894.0	1,013.6	305.2
1978	835.4	916.0	349.1
1979	875.0	965.3	402.5
1980	1,239.8	1,100.6	515.1
1981	1,130.4	1,410.3	527.3

Source: Thomas, 1982, p. 24

Real per capita GDP in 1983 was below that of 1970 and it is now questioned whether Guyana should still be considered together with Barbados (1981 per capita GDP, US$3,627), Belize (1981, US$1,066), Jamaica (1981, US$1,307), and Trinidad and Tobago (1980, US$5,783) as one of the more developed countries of the Caribbean Community, when, in 1981, its per capita GDP, at US$629, was the lowest for the entire Community (*Handbook of IT&DS*, 1984). At a figure of around US$1.23bn. Guyana has one of the highest per capita external debt rates in the world. Total public debt has grown from G$267.2m. in 1970 (US$1.00 = G$4.25, December 1984) to an estimated G$6.5b. in 1984 (Bank of Guyana, 1984).

The expansion of Government expenditure and an ever-widening deficit have been the basic policy responses to the deteriorating economic situation. Between 1971 and 1975 the central Government's deficit averaged G$74.2m., and in the latter year stood at G$141m., while in the following five years it progressively worsened, averaging

Table 7. Visible trade (G£m)

Year	Imports	Exports	Balance
1968	219.3	229.0	+9.7
1969	235.8	252.9	17.1
1970	268.2	264.8	−3.4
1971	267.6	290.9	+23.3
1972	297.9	300.0	+2.1
1973	372.5	288.0	+84.5
1974	567.0	600.0	+33.0
1975	810.6	854.4	+43.8
1976	927.4	711.3	−216.1
1977	804.3	661.2	−143.1
1978	711.1	753.8	+42.7
1979	810.1	746.4	−63.7
1980	1,010.0	991.6	−18.4
1981	1,209.0	974.0	−235.0
1982	840.0	724.0	−116.0
1983	745.0	580.0	−165.0

Source: Bank of Guyana Reports

G$349.4m. and rising to G$591.8m. in 1981 and to just under G$700m. by 1983. During the first few years of falling export prices, when the Government saw the problem as essentially a temporary aberration, it continued to increase the money supply in the hope that it could spend its way back to prosperity. Thus, in 1975, the last year of the boom in export prices, money supply increased by 41 per cent, but it continued to rise during the following two years by 9 per cent and 23 per cent respectively. It is essentially in terms of the implication of this policy, of attempting to 'deficit finance' its way out of what was mistakenly considered to be a temporary lull in export markets, that the economic catastrophe that has gripped Guyana is most clearly seen. Although initially the growth of Government expenditure was largely covered by the substantial export earnings, and briefly by monetary expansion, it quickly became necessary to borrow, first from internal and commercial sources but increasingly from international institutions as the burden grew.

The International Monetary Fund (IMF) is Guyana's largest external creditor. Although between 1966 and 1977 ten stand-by agreements had been negotiated with the IMF, only four had been taken up. In 1978, after Guyana had introduced strong deflationary measures, including a 30 per cent cut in government expenditure, in an unsuccessful attempt to correct the worsening balance of payments, a major approach (the first) was made to the IMF and a loan, equivalent to 6.25m. Special Drawing Rights (SDRs) was arranged which was 'tied' to greater emphasis being put on demand management policies by the Government. Although this did reduce aggregate demand over the year of the Agreement by some 20 per cent in real terms, it was not to correct the 'temporary' disequilibrium in the balance of payments. In 1979 a three-year Extended Fund Facility was negotiated which included a number of requirements largely designed to limit the growth of the public sector, in return for 62.75m. SDRs. However, as it was simply more of the same medicine, the Agreement ended within a year amidst worsening conditions and a new one was agreed, in collaboration with the IMF and the World Bank; but as the Government was unable to meet the targets set it was forced to withdraw early in 1982.

Again, in April 1983, Guyana approached the IMF but negotiations were suspended after fundamental disagreement over conditions, which included a 40–60 per cent devaluation and the progressive denationalization of sugar and bauxite. The conflict which seems to have compromised the relationship on both sides down to the mid-1980s has led to an impasse, with Guyana being told to put its own house in order before financial help is forthcoming, the only result of which has been a further deterioration in Guyana's economic standing. Thus, in June 1981, the G$ was devalued from G$2.55 = US$1.00 where it had stood since 1975, to G$3.00 = US$1.00. In January 1984 it was further devalued to G$3.75 = US$1.00 and the G$ is now (January 1985) G$4.30 to the US$ on the official market, while on the flourishing black market it is traded anywhere between G$10.00 to G$15.00 for a US$1.00.

The decline in Guyana's holdings of international reserves also fully reflects the worsening economic crisis and in itself has further accentuated the problem. In 1975 net holdings stood at a record G$197.7m., but with the collapse of export prices and the ensuing economic decline they fell to —G$99.8m. in 1977, —G$396.4m. in 1980 and —G$867.4m. at the end of 1983. The full implications of this are demonstrated by the fact that whereas in 1975 gross international reserves could pay for 3.3 months of imports, by 1981 this had fallen dramatically to the equivalent of one week.

The pattern of Guyana's visible trade provides an indication of her general predicament as the narrowness of the export base has made the economy particularly vulnerable to declining demand for primary products. Although Guyana has been a member of the Caribbean Free Trade Area since 1967 and Caricom since 1973 her major trading partners are the developed industrial countries. Thus, in 1983, over 80 per cent of her exports went to North America, Western Europe and Japan, in return for 54 per cent of her imports, though the major single source of imports (42 per cent) was oil from Trinidad and Tobago. The deterioration of the visible trade balance from a surplus of G$23.2m. in 1971 to a deficit of G$235m. in 1981 was partly the result of the slowing down of economic growth in the industrial countries and the growing reliance of Guyana upon vital imports. In 1983 the import bill absorbed 70 per cent of GDP (83 per cent in 1982) and this has contributed significantly to the country's growing indebtedness. In the second half of 1984 28 per cent of the country's total foreign exchange earnings went to servicing debts owed to the IMF and it is estimated that approximately one-third of Guyana's 'hard' currency receipts in 1985 will go the Fund (Budget, 1985, pp. 82–3).

The general economic situation, coupled with the dictates of the IMF, have resulted in heavy retrenchment, higher prices and widespread shortages: even of those items which are produced locally (*The Food Crisis in Guyana*, 1984). Official employment statistics are difficult to come by but some estimates put unemployment as high as 40 per cent of the working population. According to a report of the Inter-American Development Bank:

Official estimates of employment and unemployment in Guyana are not available but the economic decline clearly had a major impact on the employment situation. . . . Between late 1981 and mid 1982, the government sacked . . . 17% of the labour force. At the same time the state-owned corporations sacked an additional 7,000, mainly from the bauxite, sugar and rice industries. By year end alone . . . these cut-backs resulted in significant increases in the already high level of unemployment . . . thus generating mounting social pressure. [GIB, June, 1984, p. 1.]

The shortages affect every area of life. Food marches are not uncommon and the black market is a daily protest against an unpopular and distinctly irrational policy of self-reliance. Few would want to deny that if countries are to develop they must make the most of the indigenous resource base, but the notion of self-reliance can be taken to absurd lengths. Take, for example, the banning of wheaten flour in Guyana.

From time immemorial this item has been an intrinsic part of the daily diet of the vast majority of people and they resent the Government's restriction. Indeed, notwithstanding the ban, wheaten bread is openly sold on the black market and is periodically confiscated by the police. The Government explanation for this unpopular act is that the people must learn to eat what they produce if Guyana is to develop. So, without much success, it has gone to great lengths to make rice flour acceptable to the populace. What is most surprising about this decision is that wheat, which was imported to be ground into flour, is less expensive than rice on the world market. For example, in 1960 rice was US$125 per metric ton and wheat was US$61. In 1982 when this policy came into practice, the price of rice was relatively low, but it was still US$132 per ton more than that of wheat. It may be that the Government could not sell the rice it produced, either because it failed to find markets or because the quality of the rice it uses to make flour is low, but no such explanation has ever been given. Therefore, the regime's policy of self-reliance appears to make it impossible for it to benefit from the advantages of trade.

These problems have led to mass migration and a wave of crime. One international comparison shows Guyana second only to Lebanon in terms of crimes committed per head of population. In the United States the figure is one crime for every 20.4 persons, in Trinidad and Tobago one crime for every 20.3 persons, but in Guyana the figure is one crime for every 6.3 persons. (GIB, July, 1984, p. 1). It was estimated that while in 1970 5,000 persons emigrated, in 1980 14,000 did so (Thomas, 1982, p. 45). In 1983 there was a 62 per cent increase in new passports over the previous year, from 28,844 to 43,947, and it has been calculated that a third of the population hold some form of travel document (GIB, July, 1984, p. 3). When migration is placed against the average annual population growth of about 2.5 per cent, the population was no more than 800,000 in 1984. The resultant loss in labour force, skilled and unskilled, and in the potential consumer market, is obvious.

The nature of, and proposed solutions to, the economic crisis

At the fifth congress of the PNC in 1983, Burnham, presented the following analysis of the situation. The countries of the South, he said, were still in stagnation and decline and even the oil producers, such as Trinidad and Tobago, and the newly industrialized countries, such as Brazil and Mexico, had not benefited from improvements in the international economy which were said to have occurred in the North. The debt burden of the South had risen from US$465b. in 1980 to US$626b. in 1982, while lending had decreased and had become more politicized. Low prices for primary products, such as those produced by Guyana, protectionism and disadvantageous terms of trade were responsible for the plight of the Third World. 'Guyana's predicament is not unique. And be it understood that the developed world dictates the price of its own exports and those of our exports' (Burnham, 1983, p. 3). According to Burnham, there was little use in pleading with the North to change the international economic order and he asserted that the Third World must develop 'collective self-reliance' at global, regional and national levels. In terms of Guyana that meant that local resources must be used to fulfil local needs. 'Of course, another vital political decision has to be taken and that is that we eat our own food primarily, and not be slaves to other people's tastes.' (ibid., p. 5). The absurd lengths to which this policy of self-reliance is carried has already been shown. What is much more interesting perhaps is that this talk of the importance of agricultural development has been around for some considerable time (*To Feed the Nation*, 1973), with few practical results.

Table 8. Terms of Trade
Index

Period	Index
1970	127
1971	126
1972	135
1973	115
1974	156
1975	198
1976	123
1977	126
1978	113
1979	98
1980	100
1981	98
1982	98

Source: Handbook of IT&DS, 1984

The 1972–76 Development Plan asserted the Government's intention of feeding, clothing and housing the nation by the end of the plan period. Not even the regime could pretend that the nation is now clothing itself in any appreciable way. In aggregate terms, total consumer imports per capita increased by only 5 per cent when 1982 is compared with 1970, though per capita spending on the import of clothing increased 100 per cent (calculated from Bank of Guyana figures, 1985). The plan also stated that 65,000 housing units would be built by the end of 1976, and although the regime continues to claim that thousands of units were built, exact figures have not been produced and prominent trade unionists have estimated that only 6,000 were built by 1976 (*Roraima Journal*, 1977, pp. 5–6).

The decline in material standards is clearly seen when the most glaring of the failures of the 1972 pledges is considered. The promise to feed the nation has proved to be the most elusive of commitments. Although absolute hunger is not a widespread problem, at least up to the mid-1980s, both the quantity and quality of food supply has markedly deteriorated, and given Guyana's resource base and its

Table 9. Annual average growth rates of total and per capita food production

Countries	Total Food Production			Per Capita Food Production		
	1967/70	1970/80	1981/82	1967/70	1970/80	1981/82
Barbados	−4.6	0.3	−3.6	−5.0	−0.3	−4.4
Belize	4.3	3.7	6.4	1.6	0.6	3.3
Guyana	2.7	1.2	−1.2	0.4	−1.1	−3.3
Jamaica	−1.9	0.4	3.0	−3.1	−1.2	1.5
Trinidad and Tobago	4.0	−3.2	−3.3	3.1	−4.2	−4.3

Source: Handbook of IT&DS, 1984

tradition of food production, this is a particularly worrying problem. Thus, numerous items for long assumed to be part of the standard Guyanese diet have become increasingly scarce and unavailable to many since the mid-1970s. Basic items like flour, salt, milk, chicken, eggs and butter have all but disappeared from most families' tables as the standard of nutrition has taken a nosedive. Even though rice production has been stepped up to compensate for the 'unnecessary' importations of wheat, banned since 1982, the output of rice has failed to respond to the situation and in 1980 only 144,000 tons were produced, compared with 171,000 tons in 1980 and 219,000 tons in 1977. A major problem has been the smuggling of rice out of the country by producers in search of higher prices than those allowed by the government regulations. But a fallacy seems to exist here as rice is able to attract higher prices in the world market than the banned wheat can sustain.

Many of the most productive food producing areas have suffered substantial decline for a variety of reasons but particularly as a result of the anti-agricultural policy which the Government seemingly followed during the late 1960s and the 1970s. This saw the economic system increasingly reduce both the direct and indirect support and the incentives it gave to agriculture. Official prices for many products were lower in the early 1970s than in the mid-1960s, even though inflation had increased monetary values. A shift in the emphasis of investment away from drainage and irrigation schemes to less directly productive

infrastructure weakened the development of both rice and sugar cultivation and also the small-scale mixed farming which complemented
the agriculture of the coastal plain. The transportation of produce from
specialized farming areas such as the Rupununi has deteriorated and by
the early 1980s the number of animals slaughtered was less than half
the peak years of the mid-1970s.

Most of the formerly active land development schemes have, by the
mid-1980s, fallen into disuse, while the local government authorities
do virtually nothing in the way of maintenance of existing infrastructure. Further, the introduction of political bias into the distribution of land and the failure of the Government to ensure consistent
pricing and marketing strategies have made for an unstable agricultural
context which has further diminished the production endeavours of
most groups of farmers. Indeed, even by 1976, when all Guyanese
'would be adequately fed' food consumption was at a chronically low
level and the average intake of the majority of the population included
only 1 egg, 7oz of fish, 4oz of beef and 2lb of ground provisions per
week and by the middle of the 1980s many of these previously standard
items were largely unobtainable.

Although fish and shrimps had traditionally provided an important
component of the average diet, the burden of high costs on the small
fishermen, the major suppliers of the general population, especially the
ever-increasing licence fees, have severely reduced their significance. In
addition, because of the various difficulties faced by rice growers, even
consumption of this basic staple has suffered periodic shortages. Thus,
from a position of plenty in the 1960s when Guyanese people benefited
from a productively efficient agriculture, dietary standards have
rapidly declined and in the mid-1980s the hitherto unlikely problem of
malnutrition looms large. Perhaps a fitting postscript to this predicament is the fact that in 1982 the average consumption of meat was
3.5lb for the year.

While not denying that the factors Mr Burnham identified
adversely affected the economy, other commentators have placed more
emphasis on the failings of internal productive capacity.

Stagnation and decline in production and productivity have led to a grave
economic and financial crisis which is manifested in serious balance of

payments and budgetary deficits, which the state is attempting to resolve by deficit financing. The consequence of deficit financing, anti-working people's fiscal measures and rampant inflation has been a rapid deterioration of living standards and is closely interlinked with the social crisis. [*For Socialism in Guyana*, 1982, p. 37.]

As already indicated, people in the regime closely connected with economic management accept that production is the basic problem. In presenting the 1982 budget, the Vice-President for Economic Planning and Finance stated: 'To put it bluntly, the performance of our economy in 1981 was disastrous. Physical output was unacceptably low and in consequence financial outturn disappointed' (Budget, 1982, p. 17). Further, the 1985 Budget seems to have recognized the causal implications fully, in stating that: 'this is imperative given that our ability to physically determine production and distribution is still not well developed. We are inevitably forced to rely on modified and unmodified market mechanisms to perform many of the resource allocative functions' (Budget, 1985, pp. 9–10). Rice, sugar and bauxite still account for 75 per cent of Guyana's export earnings and it does not take great insight to recognize that the lesson of Table 5 is one of stagnation and decline. The ability of the productive capacity of Guyana's three basic commodities to respond effectively to changing market forces is therefore a vital determinant of prosperity.

Both sugar growing and processing underwent significant rationalization in the two decades or so after the Second World War and the large-scale mechanization led to the unbridled displacement of thousands of workers at a time when unemployment was already a serious problem. Between 1947 and 1975 the industry's labour force declined from over 30,000 to 17,000, with field work becoming almost as capital intensive as factories and between 1950 and 1971 the number of field workers fell from 21,641 to 14,447 and factory workers from 6,594 to 3,074. As a result, in the years leading up to nationalization, the industry was in a healthy productive position and substantial returns were being enjoyed as world markets expressed a seemingly insatiable demand for Guyana's sugar. In 1976, however, when the Guyana Sugar Corporation (Guysuco) was established, the boom in the world sugar prices was coming to an end and the industry's future was to be a far from sure one.

The peak year in the industry was 1971, when 369,000 tons of sugar were produced, but since then and even during the rest of the early 1970s output has consistently failed to reach that level. Indeed, after 1976 when the boom in world prices ended, the trend in output has been consistently downwards, though annual figures have varied quite widely. Most estimates agree that the sugar industry could run at around 450,000 tons full annual capacity, so that since the mid-1970s it has performed at between 50 per cent and 70 per cent of its potential. No longer protected by a buoyant market, the industry was exposed to a series of productive and organizational difficulties which compounded the situation and led to further deterioration. In particular, the failure to improve on standards of crop husbandry must stand as the central problem, though this has been seen as a function of other less predictable difficulties. Thus, despite the fact that although two harvesting seasons are possible every year (January–May and July–December), the sucrose content of Guyanese cane is so poor, owing to the high humidity which impairs the ripening process, that the yields remain at a chronically low level. More land, resources and effort have therefore to be put into each ton of Guyana's sugar than for most of her competitors. Indeed, this predicament has deteriorated over the years and one estimate puts the yield of sugar per acre in 1980 at 2.23 tons, compared to a yield of 2.94 tons in 1970. As 108,885 acres of cane were cultivated in 1980, the drop in efficiency would have represented a loss of just over 76,000 tons of sugar, or G$84.9m. at 1980 prices. Indeed, the actual output in 1980 was just over half of the target of 500,000 tons which the Government had predicted as early as 1971 (*The Food Crisis in Guyana*, 1984).

The declining productivity of the industry was not simply the result of poor physical conditions, although these played a part. Both the decline in the yields of canes per acre and of sugar per cane were accentuated by Guyana's inability to secure adequate supplies of inputs vital to the industry's progress. Insufficient amounts of fertilizer and other agro-chemicals, the paucity of spare parts for the processing machinery and the failure to keep up with technological improvements, both in the factory and in the field, were all the result of the worsening foreign exchange situation. In addition, the state of the industry's labour relations has been far from conducive to stable productive growth. In

1975, 1977 and 1979 major strikes largely accounted for the lower production levels which occurred and although the 1975 strikes led to the recognition of the GAWU, the sugar industry has paid a considerable price ever since, as Guysuco and GAWU have maintained a veritable stalemate.

Table 10. Indices of physical output of selected commodities—annual rates

Commodities	Physical output in /72 000, tons	1971	1972	1973	1974	1977	1980	1983
Sugar	315	117.1	100	84.1	108.2	76.8	85.6	79.9
Rice	94	127.7	100	117.0	152.1	223.5	176.6	154.5
Bauxite:								
Dried	1,652	127.6	100	100.7	83.0	61.6	58.2	42.6
Calcined	690	102.9	100	92.3	105.2	104.3	87.1	40.0
Aluminia	257	118.7	100	91.1	121.0	107.8	83.7	—

— not available
Source: Bank of Guyana, 1985

Although some improvements have taken place, such as more systematic planting and harvesting programmes and improved drainage, their combined impact has been limited. Declining yields of cane per acre, and particularly of sugar per cane, are more reflective of the true state of the industry. Thus, between 1970 and 1983, whereas the yields of cane per acre fluctuated, though on a downward trend from 34.8 tons to 30.1 tons, the yield of sugar per acre has fallen consistently from 2.9 tons to 2.1 tons. In the light of these circumstances and of the contrasting and changing world market it is surprising that Guyana has largely failed, either to consciously reduce the rural economy's dependence upon sugar, or to diversify substantially into by-products processing much beyond the distillation of rum. Very little white sugar is manufactured, for example, since traditional Demerara has dominated. The world's demand for sugar has for long provided Guyana with substantial foreign earnings, but never on a secure basis and the declining competitiveness of the industry (Guyana has experienced repeated difficulties in meeting its Lome Convention quotas, for instance), coupled with world over-production has made this a far less profitable source. Indeed, during the first six years of nationalization, 1976–81, Guysuco made a mere G$13m. profit, less than half the amount paid in compensation to the former owners during the same period. Perhaps the postscript to Guyana's predicament is just being written, in mid-1985, with the EEC's dumping of heavily subsidized beet sugar on the world market, an action which has pushed the price down to G$186 a metric ton, less than half that of twelve months earlier and well below the average cost of production in Guyana.

Bauxite, Guyana's other major export earner, has also suffered from both declining demand and a weak and deteriorating production function in the years since 1976 when the Guyana Mining Enterprise Ltd (Guymine) was established. As with sugar, the problem has largely manifested itself in productive over-capacity as available resources have been consistently under-utilized. In 1977 reserves were put at 150m. tons, but a more recent survey of West Guyana has indicated much greater levels in the Pakarima Plateau region where the new East Montgomery mine is expected to produce 50 per cent of total annual output of calcined bauxite by 1989. In addition, the new Kwakwini mine promises to increase production significantly and, along with the granting of a G$186m. government loan to modernize production, to improve the quality of the most profitable product, calcined bauxite, and to help clear Guymine's overdraft with private banks, the industry's productive potential seemingly looks healthier. Indeed, it was the only sector to show some significant growth in 1984, after years of decline, thus helping to give Guyana a 2 per cent growth rate (Budget, 1985).

But the lost opportunities of the first decade of nationalization might never be recaptured and have probably left an indelible blemish on the industry's future. The production of bauxite fell from the high levels of the 1970s which averaged around 3.5m. tons, to 1.8m. tons in 1980, 2.1m. tons in 1981, 1.4m. tons in 1982 (a mere half of target) and to just over 1m. tons in 1983. The comparative decline in the production of different grades is shown by the index of physical output (Table 10) based on 1972. In 1982 the respective outputs were: dried bauxite 45.5, calcined bauxite 56.1 and aluminia 27.9. Although high profits were made by Guymine throughout the 1970s, the last profit was in 1979—G$51m., after which the position has successively deteriorated, with losses recorded in 1982—G$153m., and 1983—G$131m. As virtually all the bauxite went for export, not only did this see a decline in the industry's commercial viability, but also a significant contraction in Guyana's major source of foreign exchange. Although the output of most grades of bauxite has fallen, it is calcined bauxite which has suffered most and although Guyana is still the world's major producer, her market share fell from 85 to 57 per cent between 1975 and 1984 as increased supplies, especially from China, began to flood world markets.

As with sugar, bauxite has also suffered from production difficulties which have persistently inhibited the ability of the industry to respond effectively to changing market forces. The scarcity of vital inputs, a weak managerial structure and the frequent labour unrest have all combined to reduce productive potential. The markets for most grades of Guyana's bauxite have, in turn, shrunk, as the reliability of the industry has become increasingly more suspect. Thus, although calcined bauxite is the preferred material in the manufacture of refractory products, inroads into the market have been made by suppliers of inferior ore which has caused customers to adapt their technologies, while substitute products such as the South African metal ore, andalusite, have further narrowed demand. The world recession has resulted in a significant cutback in demand for aluminium, with a consequent reduction in sales of metal grade bauxite, though the agreements made in 1983 to supply the USSR and Venezuela have certainly improved prospects.

Perhaps the fact that Guymine is competing in a world market dominated by a few giant multinational firms has been too great a burden to bear, particularly through a world recession. With all of Guymine's eggs in one, or rather two, baskets—Linden and Kwakwini—the industry has been unable to move from the problems which come with such narrow productive arrangements. Certainly, the future of Guyana's bauxite industry looks brighter than its recent past might suggest in the light of the resource potential which is being developed in the mid-1980s. The big question, however, is whether the industry will be able to effectively respond to the challenge and solve the many niggling problems which continue to reduce productive efficiency.

The cultivation of rice has for long provided the population's staple diet; its annual consumption per capita is among the world's highest— 90 kilos per person—and it is a dependable earner of foreign exchange. It is also a key component of the rural economy and provides a living for nearly 50,000 families. Although the farms vary in size from half an acre to 1,000 acres, the vast majority are small, though the few large producers are highly mechanized and thus contribute disproportionately to total output. Overall, productivity is low, however, as the majority of rice farmers work part time.

In 1975 a large-scale irrigation scheme was commenced at Tapakuma in the Essequibo region which, together with the Mahaica-Mahaicony river drainage and irrigation projects was designed to substantially increase the potential for rice cultivation. The first stage was completed in 1983 and in early 1984, despite American attempts to veto it, the World Bank gave further aid of US$40.7m. to expand the project which will bring into production a total of 37,000 acres of riceland. The rice industry is privately run but the Government, through the Guyana Rice Board, operates a scheme which finances rice farmers to buy fertilizers and to hire ploughing, reaping and harvesting services. However, the Government's inconsistent approach has resulted in shortages of a range of necessary inputs including fertilizers, insecticides, bags and cutlasses which, together with the chronically low prices received by the farmers in most years, have seen output fluctuating widely and a resultant instability in the production of the population's staple food and an important source of foreign exchange. Between 1979 and 1983 annual output varied from 136,000, to 171,000, to 168,000, to 182,000 and to 144,000 tonnes. Thus, despite some improvements in recent years, rice production has not seen a significant expansion.

Because of their overall significance, sugar, rice and bauxite were collectively responsible for just under 40 per cent of GNP during the 1970s and early 1980s; most other economic activities have also suffered hard times, though many have contributed substantially to their own shortcomings. Thus, although Guyana's fishing industry employs over

5,000 and is the main exporter (mainly shellfish) in the Caribbean, there has been no attempt made to can or otherwise process fish and Guyana has thus virtually subsidized customers who have themselves undertaken the profitable processing activities. Again, although Guyana has some 20,000 square miles of exploitable forest and the Upper Demerara Forestry Project is planned to raise timber output by 70 per cent, little has been done thus far to develop the extensive resources, or to establish viable by-product and processing units. Although the mining of gold and diamonds brings a rich bonus to the exchequer, an almost equivalent value is thought to be smuggled out of the country illegally. Indeed, the failure of Guyana to sufficiently realize its resource potential can be seen as a central failing of its economic make-up and, together with the negative multiplier effects that the unstable behaviour of the 'commanding heights' generate, explains the supply side of the economic predicament.

The production problems did not occur in a vacuum, however, and the failure of the Government to create and sustain an environment conducive to healthy economic growth must be seen as the root cause of Guyana's relatively poor performance. Professor Clive Thomas has argued that the crisis was caused primarily by mismanagement which was brought on by the unplanned nature of government activities; the shortage of skilled personnel caused by migration; insufficient finance which has led to poor maintenance of the productive capacity; frequent breakdowns of public utilities such as water, electricity and transport the collapse of social services and political discrmination and victimization of workers which has led to the alienation of the work-force According to Professor Thomas, bureaucratic restraints intended to rationalize this situation produce negative results. These unite to create a vicious circle of decreasing production (Thomas, 1982, pp. 45–6).

Thomas saw the answer in the all-round democratization of production and consumption. He argued that, 'Workers' democracy cannot exist without [political] democracy and representative institutions in other spheres of social life. At the minimum, therefore, such political changes must represent the will of the masses.' (Ibid., 1982 pp. 63–4.) Therefore, although Thomas posits a production crisis leading to a general crisis, he sees the solution in essentially political terms. The official opposition also wants a political solution.

We said this long ago. There could be no solution to the economic and social crisis without a solution to the political crisis.... The superstructure caused the economy to go down, and now the economy is affecting the super-structure. Unless you make fundamental changes at the superstructural level, in politics, in ideology, in culture,... you cannot solve this problem. [*Guyana Crisis; Bankruptcy; Solution*, 1982, pp. 57–8.]

The political solution and the economic crisis

The regime has accepted that there is a production problem and it also acknowledges that there has been much mismanagement at the enter-prise level. For example, in 1982, the Vice-President for Economic Planning and Finance admitted that there had been severe managerial failures in the bauxite industry. He went on to argue that:

the most serious problem facing the industry is the fact that it has lost its near monopoly of the supply of calcined bauxite to the world market. In large measure, it is attributable to our own default. During the years 1977 to 1979, in particular, primarily because of low production, the industry was unable to satisfy the market demand for calcined bauxite, and this circumstance presented an opportunity for the entry of competitors into the refractory market.... Thus the challenge to the industry is to improve reliability of supply and cost efficiency. [Budget, 1982, pp. 22–3.]

But even in terms of the wider economy, the regime has not made adequate use of the opportunities which are open to it. To take one simple example: Guyana has productive fishing grounds which are used by other countries and almost a decade and a half after the Government banned all canned fish imports it has not been able to provide such a product. The technology is relatively simple and, given the substantial local demand which exists, such an industry could have provided real employment and export opportunities but nothing has been done. The Third Development Plan targeted a 17 per cent growth in the economy for the four years 1978–81. The actual 'achievements' starkly evidenced this inefficiency even at the level of planning: 1978, 0 per cent; 1979, −2 per cent; 1980, +2 per cent; 1981, −0.5 per cent. The Plan's progress was replete with failures and under-achievements and so the balance of payments current account deficit which was to be reduced to G$59m. by 1981 increased to G$558m. Bauxite sales which were planned to exceed G$600m. by 1981 were G$428m. Therefore, mismanagement can be seen to exist at both the micro and macro levels and its roots are to be located in the colonial political solution where race and geopolitics served to install and perpetuate the PNC in Government.

Political conditions have made it possible for the PNC to hang on to power irrespective of the level of its mismanagement or the unpopularity of its policies. Furthermore, since the regime is unaccountable, the pressure on it to perform is paradoxically less than it might have been. This is a crucial factor when the state controls most of the economy. Indeed, so long as the regime could satisfy the demands of its supporters there was absolutely no urgency for it to come to grips with the declining rates of production of which it was made aware very early on (*Roraima Journal*, 1977, pp. 1–19). Even in its ideological commitment to co-operation, upon which it has continued to place much verbal emphasis, the PNC has not felt obliged to perform.

In 1970 Guyana was declared a Co-operative Republic but the PNC first committed itself to co-operation as early as 1961, when it was the official opposition party (Burnham, 1970, pp. 11–12), and the present constitution of the country states that:

Co-operativism in practice shall be the dynamic principle of socialist transformation and shall pervade and inform all interrelationships in the society. Co-operativism is rooted in the historical experience of the people, is based on self-reliance, is capable of releasing the productive energies of the people, and is a unifying principle in the total development of the nation. [*Constitution of Guyana*, 1980, p. 23.]

However, there is a significant conceptual difference between the theory as it was first proposed and as it now stands.

As it was first conceptualized, co-operation had two essential dimensions. Firstly, the primitive communalistic existence of the indigenous Amerindian peoples; the attempts which were made by the newly emancipated slaves to organize peasant villages based upon some features of modern co-operation; the many efforts at collective work and saving which litter Guyanese history and the substantial legacy of modern co-operation which dates from the first decade of this century are all advanced as evidence of a general desire on the part of the Guyanese people to work together for the common good (Dowden, 1971; Grant, 1975; *Speakers Brief*, No. 10, 1980, p. 89). The second dimension is found in the decision to develop the traditional co-operative societies into the dominant sector of the economy. In commemorating the declaration of the Co-operative Republic, Burnham argued thus:

A distinction must be drawn between the Co-operative as we envisage it in the Co-operative Republic and the Co-operative as it exists in the West and in the East. In the West the Co-operative is peripheral to the capitalist system . . . In the East again the Co-operative is peripheral to a given system which is entirely under the control of a group of men from whom all orders . . . flow . . . We should hope and expect that the Co-operative will become a major sector, in fact the major sector of the economy of Guyana. [Burnham, 1970b, pp. 14–16.]

Although the extent of co-operative organization has varied between different sectors of the economy, it has nowhere predominated. Thus, at the end of 1983 there were only 1,522 small co-operative societies in Guyana and around a quarter of this number were School Thrift Societies. There were 104 Industrial Co-operatives, with an average of twenty-five members. Cane farming societies were among the most financially successful agricultural co-operatives in 1983 but the twenty societies only accounted for 3 per cent of total sugar production (*Annual Report*, 1983). Figures have not been given for the total membership and share capital of the co-operative sector but estimates by people close to the movement place them at no more than 140,000 persons and G$75m. But the vast majority of members are either in societies which are inactive or are schoolchildren.

Further, even those sectors in which co-operative forms have been officially created, such as the Guyana National Co-operative Bank, or the Guyana Co-operative Insurance Company, are invariably operated along straightforward capitalist lines, as are most of the successful privately organized co-operatives. There are also many modifications to and deviations from co-operative principles: many organize simply to be eligible for the substantial tax concessions which are offered to co-operatives, some make liberal use of wage labour and still others are formed for strictly commercial reasons, such as the land societies which receive land grants from the state while their members proceed to farm independently. Twenty years after independence and fifteen after the declaration of a Co-operative Republic, the co-operative movement remains weak and insignificant and a long way from the expectations of 1961.

A weak co-operative movement, coupled with state ownership of 80 per cent of the economy and the regime's commitment to Marxist-Leninism (Burnham, 1976) raised certain conceptual difficulties which demanded a reconceptualization of the co-operative ideology. For example, if the co-operative sector was to be the dominant sector as the regime insisted, then were the newly nationalized industries to be sold to private individuals organized in co-operative socities and, if so, how did this relate to the Marxist demand for social ownership and control of, at least, the major means of production?

By 1980 the PNC was ready with its new conceptualization which took the emphasis away from the development of the traditional co-operative societies and placed it on the application of international co-operative principles. As it is to be applied in Guyana, the ideology of co-operation now has three distinct aspects: the two already discussed and a third which envisages the maintenance of national ownership in the state sector but seeks to democratize state enterprises by co-operativizing the decision-making process within them. 'The idea is to allow all non-capitalist groups in the society, whose interests are fundamentally affected by the operations of the institution, some control over the operations of that institution' (*Co-operativism*, 1980, p. 12). The policy paper on co-operativism projected that controlling arrangements comprising such groups as the workers of an enterprise, the consumers of the product of the enterprise, representatives of the community in which the enterprise is located and government and trade union representatives, could be devised to govern given enterprises. Democratic structures based upon the principles outlined above were considered sufficient for the development of socialism in Guyana (Ibid., pp. 14–22). We do not wish to deny these possibilities, but what is significant is that, notwithstanding its rhetoric, the regime has not felt compelled to either develop the traditional co-operative sector or to democratize the state sector as proposed.

The massive excitement which followed independence in the late

1960s and the buoyant prices for exports in the first half of the 1970s disguised a political factor which was already having a direct impact on the level of production, particularly in the agricultural sectors of rice and sugar production where PPP supporters are dominant.

To take the sugar industry as an example: after the British changed the constitution in 1963, the PPP, bent on demonstrating that it remained a force to be reckoned with, called upon its union, GAWU, which was not then the recognized union in the industry, to step up its demand for recognition. The result was that hundreds of acres of cane were destroyed by arson and the tonnage of sugar produced that year was the lowest for the decade. Production levels in election years are good indicators of how the PPP has continued to affect the economy. The 280,000 tons of sugar produced in the election year of 1973 was the second lowest output for that decade, only better than the 253,000 tons produced in 1977, when the GAWU called a strike for profit sharing, which the government claimed was a political strike intended to remove it from office (Burnham, 1979, pp. 11–14). In the election year of 1980 production was only marginally better than in 1973. We have previously mentioned that of the 653 strikes called in Guyana in 1982 the GAWA called 639. The colonial solution did not satisfy the PPP and so it continues to make a very expensive point.

As indicated above, the second half of the 1970s was a bad time for the regime: high inflation, falling prices for its exports, but most of all low production due to mismanagement, lost opportunities, unaccountable government and political disaffection, sent it scurrying to the IMF and this meant that it had to be prepared to swallow the traditional deflationary medicine (Burnham, 1978). The result was that the regime was now compelled to attack its traditional supporters: it was forced to carry out mass retrenchment in the state bureaucracy, precisely where most of them were employed. It had to cut subsidies on numerous food items and intensify its rather dubious notion of self-reliance, which led to it banning such basic items as wheat flour. Urban dwellers, who normally have to purchase most of their food needs, were the hardest hit, but it was precisely in the urban areas that the PNC's support had been greatest. Faced with this dilemma, the party started a campaign to encourage people in the urban areas to plant every empty plot of land with a food crop.

In strictly economic terms, then, by the middle of the 1980s, after nearly two decades of independence, Guyana has, despite its socialist intentions, or perhaps because of them, suffered productive failures and financial hardships which have been exaggerated by the undue dependence upon international market relations. Although the productive weaknesses can, as Professor Thomas has shown, be presented as a comprehensive explanation of economic failure in its own right, this is seen as inadequate in the light of Guyana's continued reliance upon external market forces. Economic realism suggests that given the constraints inherited from its colonial past, once the ruling party determined that Guyana should continue to earn its living and, more curiously, attempt to construct a radical socialism within capitalist market relations, the die was cast. Over the past twenty years the fluctuating interaction of changing market forces has resulted in an economic climate which aggravated the simmering political crisis and the latter then began to exacerbate the economic difficulties. The current crisis in Guyana, therefore, has its roots in the undemocratic nature of government, which is part and parcel of that colonial political solution which sought to replace a communist orientated regime which did not tally with Western capitalist interests. The disfranchisement of the entire people and the political alienation of the majority ultimately translated themselves into stagnation and decline which led to mass frustration. The demand for a political solution to the present crisis is a recognition that the colonial solution has failed and that a national consensus has to be reached and perennially restated if the nation is to develop. The difficulty with this thesis is that the PPP, now more communist than ever (*For Socialism in Guyana*, 1982), is still a force to be reckoned with and, particularly on the American continent, the priorities of international capital have not changed.

9 Domestic and Foreign Policy

Domestic policies

Education

Opponents of the regime claim that at no point in the history of Guyana has the education system regressed at its present rate.

The system is beset with problems resulting from mismanagement, poor planning and lack of interest in the needs of the children. Besides the problems of insufficient textbooks, audio-visual aids, science laboratories and equipment, lack of accommodation and other fundamental requisites of the system, there are also the perennial problems of overcrowding and under-staffing, and inadequate or non-existing sanitary and water facilities. [*Women's Struggle*, 1983, p. 25.]

There is undoubtedly a general belief that the education system is in disarray and this is extremely sad since education has been one of the areas in which the PNC, and Burnham in particular, has shown par-ticular interest. Part of the problem results from the weak economic situation but there has also been poor planning and co-ordination.

In his 1975 speech to the Congress of his party, Burnham gave two reasons why the party must pay particular attention to education. Firstly, he argued, Guyana cannot be developed without adequate skilled manpower, which means that educational opportunites must be provided to all Guyanese if the nation is to make best use of its human resources. Secondly, he claimed that a socialist party is automatically committed to equality of opportunity in education as in all other fields (Burnham, 1975, p. 26).

Elsewhere, the party leadership has argued that equality in the field of education is the basis of social equality. Furthermore, like most socialists, Burnham and his colleagues believed that the ultimate success of socialism depends upon the creation of a new socialist man and they saw education as having a special contribution to make in his creation.

Finally, most of the leading members of the PNC are from the lower sections of the colonial Creole middle class whose parents were school-teachers and many, like Burnham, Reid and Hoyte, were teachers themselves and made their way because they were able to take advantage of educational opportunities.

But although a belief in the power of education comes easily to this group, it holds a mechanistic concept of teaching and learning. One becomes educated by working with those who know or by being taught by those who know. One searches in vain for a conceptualization which recognizes the dialectic between theory and practice which is so important to the Marxist notion of the development of socialist man. The PNC sees no problematic in the question 'who shall educate the educators?' As a result it has not developed an approach to deal with it. The leadership assume that they are already sufficiently knowledgeable to be the educators. Thus, on the question of workers' control, the leadership of the party is never tired of arguing that workers' control will be allowed when the workers are sufficiently educated, as if, in this kind of situation, the workers will ever become educated enough without having been given the opportunity to manage. Of course, we are aware that the regime may be rationalizing its reluctance to allow workers' control, fearing that it could lead to the opposition gaining a controlling influence over important industries. However, the very fact that the maintainance of the colonial relations of production is defended in this way provides us with an insight into how the education process is viewed.

The Government has carried out structural changes to the education system and even its opponents would find it hard to deny that the theory and general direction of practice have been progressive. By the end of the 1960s the regime had begun to reorganize the education system to make it more relevant to national and local needs. A system of community high and multilateral secondary schools was introduced to provide comprehensive secondary education in the traditional subjects and in non-traditional areas such as agriculture, arts and crafts, mechanics and home economics. In 1973 a paramilitary organization, the Guyana National Service (GNS), was established and since the Government likes to stress the Service's educational rather than military objectives, we will consider it here. According to the State

Paper which preceded the establishment of the GNS, the Government saw it as an institution capable of producing cadres with the requisite skills to enable them to break away from the coast and move to the hinterland where, it claims, the future of the nation rests. National service was intended to do the following:

1. Prepare Guyanese to utilise their time and energies profitably and productively.
2. Equip them with the knowledge and experience for opening up, developing and living on the rich lands available in our hinterland.
3. Mobilise and motivate support for our thrust to 'Feed, Clothe and House' ourselves.
4. Develop the necessary skills and attitudes which go with and into nation building and national development.
5. Transform individuals geared for depending upon external aid, into self-reliant and productive citizens.
6. Encourage the physical and mental discipline necessary for satisfactory and satisfying development.
7. Ensure cohesion and unity between the various ethnic, religious, social and economic groups in Guyana. [*Guyana National Service State Paper*, 1973.]

GNS is divided into corps providing for every age group from 8 to 25 and is an intricate part of the school system at all levels. Indeed, one of the most problematic issues has been the demand that all students at the University of Guyana, or those intending to further their education abroad on government scholarships, must serve one year of national service at one of its interior settlements or in such areas as its Secretariat may determine. There is no concrete evidence that the Service has as yet made its recruits more ready to move to the hinterland although it has provided them with a better appreciation of the nature and potentials of Guyana. Others have argued that training at GNS settlements is a waste of time for university students. Although there may be much time wasting, one gets the impression that these critics are students who resent their university courses being extended by a year, and parents who do not like the idea of their children, particularly girls, having to live for a year on the settlements. The opposition parties have usually taken a negative view of national service as presently consti-tuted. Thus, after complaining that the interpretation given to

Guyanese history in GNS lectures is a distortion of the truth and that it cannot support compulsory national service for women since it offends against the mores and customs of the Indian community, the PPP stated that:

We would support national service for men only if the harmful features are eradicated. In this regard, we propose:
1. The establishment of a Committee made up of equal members of government and opposition members to review all educational manuals, books, and other publications for use at National Service camps.
2. The setting up of committees made up of government and opposition members at each camp site, which can look into all complaints and grievances.
3. Physical culture and military training for all, irrespective of political affiliation or race.

If national service is to be made compulsory for men, in addition to the points just enunciated, we demand:
1. A fair system of recruitment on a lottery basis.
2. Equal opportunity legislation and an independent Commission to administer the Act with equal representation for government and the opposition.
[*Documents of the 19th Congress*, 1976, p. 36.]

The declaration of a Co-operative Republic in 1970 was followed in 1973 by the creation of the Kuru Kuru Co-operative College to provide managerial and general co-operative education for co-operators and the general public. In 1974 Burnham took a stronger socialist line and between then and 1978 the regime organized the Workers' Education Unit to provide ideological/labour programmes for workers at their place of work and, in 1977, the Cuffy Ideological Institute opened its doors to provide residential programmes of ideological education for people of all levels. In September 1976 the Government took over some 600 schools, about 200 of which were owned by religious organizations and free education from nursery to university was introduced. In 1979 national policy education, dealing with social and political topics, was made an examination subject at the Secondary School Entrance Examination. At that time, approximately 29,000 pupils, or 78 per cent of the eligible age-group, attended nursery schools (Chandisingh, 1979, p. 27), and 164,836 and 46,000 pupils attended primary and secondary schools respectively (*Statistical Yearbook for Latin America*, 1983). The regime has also increased the number of technical colleges and supported the expansion and development of the University of Guyana and, as can be seen from the All Items Urban Consumer Index (Table 5), expenditure on education has just about kept pace with the rate of inflation.

Table 11. Percentage enrolment in the education system by age group*

	1960	1965	1970	1975	1980	1985
6–11	90.5	94.4	88.4	83.8	95.6	98.5
12–17	62.8	66.4	62.4	61.5	65.9	76.1
18–23	4.7	6.1	7.5	8.7	10.9	12.9

* Projected to 1985
Source: Statistical Yearbook for Latin America, 1983

Although the education system could not have escaped the consequences of economic decline, the limited finances could have been better utilized. For example, in the area of ideological/labour education there are the Co-operative College, Cuffy Ideological Institute, the Workers' Education Unit and Critchlow Labour College (this is a TUC institution but is financially supported by the Government), each of them trying to do virtually the same work and each of them grossly under-utilized. Then there are the Extra-mural Department of the University of Guyana, the Extra-mural Department of the Co-operative College and the Adult Education Association, all competing in the same area. Again, everyone concerned with education is well

Table 12. Expenditure on health, education and security

	Health G\$m.	Education	Law & order	Defence
1964	6.8	11.5	6.5	1.5
1970	11.0	19.1	11.0	6.5
1974	19.1	39.0	17.6	15.9
1980	42.1	95.0	35.9	55.9
1984*	47.0	97.5	52.2	78.9

* Budget estimate
Source: Bank of Guyana Reports

aware that the economic decline and this ambitious education programme has led to a tremendous deterioration at all levels of the
system, but instead of using available resources to improve what
already exists, the regime is now building a President's College which is
intended to be the biggest and best of the secondary schools and which
most people agree is unnecessary. Guyana is a very small country and it
does not take much to see that what is necessary after two decades of *ad
hoc* but well-intentioned expansion, is for the system to be streamlined
and made more efficient. These are technical problems but there is also
a political one: teachers are part of society and so cannot avoid being
affected by the political struggle. The regime might introduce a
national policy on education but it cannot prevent the teachers from
using such sessions to propagate anti-government views, which the
social crisis helps to legitimize.

Culture

The PNC approach to culture contains three important elements: a
stress upon the need to use and develop indigenous resources, a liberal
approach to different national cultures and a belief that mass culture
should be allowed to flower and develop.

The decolonization process set in train demands for indigenous
cultural developments which led to a rejection of what was conceived
to be the culture of the colonial masters. Guyana was no exception to
this general rule and one of the first acts of the PNC Government was
to actively discourage the wearing of European-type suits and shoes as
inappropriate for the tropics. The shirt *jac* (which Jagan began to wear
after his first visit to Cuba in 1960 and for which he was asked to leave
the Legislature because he was not properly dressed) and slippers were
recommended instead. When the regime is in serious economic difficulty it attempts to justify austere economic programmes by linking
them to this aspect of its cultural approach. Thus, in the early 1970s,
before increased commodity prices had improved Guyana's balance of
payments position, the banning of many food items was justified on
the grounds that the taste for them resulted from a trading pattern
which was advantageous to the metropolitan countries but exploitative
of the colonies. The destruction of colonialism meant that the popula-

tion must develop a taste for their own resources. This policy was not pursued with any vigour once the economic situation improved but as it deteroriated again in the late 1970s and the Government was once again forced to restrict consumption, Burnham returned to the theme: 'Let us understand that the imperialists have a plan, short and long term. What better means of keeping a people subject and dependent than to dictate their tastes? "Prove" to them that it is cheaper and more economical to import food than to produce their own.' (Burnham, 1983, p. 8). Coming from a socialist this is obviously not a logical argument. Burnham has repeatedly insisted that socialism is intended to develop the whole man and all his senses. Taste is but one sense which, outside its most basic expression—sweet, sour, etc.—cannot be developed without an historical relationship to its object. That is, one will hardly develop a taste for an object if one is not familiar with it and socialism demands that we be given the opportunity to develop our taste, as one of our senses, in an all-round way. It is therefore non-sensical to imply notions of colonial taste. The PNC could argue that Third World counrtries must give priority to the development of their own resource base and thus learn to consume their own products or it may say that the nation is not as yet economically able to provide for this level of development. But, as we have repeatedly seen, the implications of the Government programmes have not been properly thought out.

Cultural liberalism is important for a country of six races and varying degrees of cultural differentiation and which has been rocked by racial strife. One of the first acts of the Government was to state its intention to legalize *obeah* (voodoo) which, it claimed, is but another form of religious expression adhered to by a section of society. Important religious occasions of the various racial/cultural groups have been made into public holidays and, where posible, other cultural groups are encouraged to take part in these events. Mashramani, which is an Amerindian celebration to mark the end of a successful co-operative effort, is now celebrated on Republic Day, 23 February, each year and the regime has tried, without much success, to promote Mashramani rather than Christmas as the main seasonal festival. These diverse cultural expressions are encouraged within a framework of unity and co-operativism, intended to be the uniting ethos of nation building.

In its narrower sense, culture, we are constantly told, is not the exclusive pursuit of the elite: working people must be given the opportunity to develop their cultural activities. In a 1972 address to the nation on the occasion of the Caribbean Festival of Creative Arts which was held in Guyana, Burnham called upon the artists participating to portray the culture of the 'small man', and returning to that theme five years later, after the completion of the National Cultural Centre, he outlined his understanding of this aspect of the cultural question. He argued that constructing a socialist state means more than economic change: it implies seeking to end man's alienation from himself and this means that the culture of the 'small man' which was frowned upon, ridiculed and even suppressed during the colonial period must be encouraged if lives are to be enriched and self-confidence attained. Socialism and suppression of the cultural forms of the people are mutually inconsistent. 'There still remains a large segment, a straight lifting of European images and imagery, but, in many areas, there has been original adaptation.' (Burnham, 1977, p. 28).

Confusion could and did arise from this conceptualization. It was obviously important to stress the need to develop indigenous cultural forms but the impression was given that only mass culture was good and that even the so-called European classical traditions should be discarded so that, for example, the steel band should be considered more culturally acceptable than a symphony orchestra. Of course, this was not the intention of the leadership and it was a ridiculous idea. After all, the world of culture belongs to all men and, as with taste, all men should have the opportunity to become involved in as much of it as possible. It is a dangerous narrowmindedness which leads to the rejection of any part of world culture without first making a conscious effort to understand and appreciate it.

Religion

Guyanese are very religious and, like people the world over, have more respect for religious than political leaders. Even in the period of feverish political activity in the 1960s it was the clarion call of the Christian Social Council to protest against the PPP's decision to take over church schools which produced one of the largest gatherings Georgetown has ever seen, when some 20,000 people assembled at

Bourda Green. Some 46 per cent of the population are Christian, 37 per cent Hindu and 8 per cent Muslim. Anglicanism is the largest Christian denomination, followed by Roman Catholicism, and there are numerous smaller churches ranging from the familiar Methodists, Presbyterians and Seven Day Adventists to the lesser-known African Coptic Church and the indigenous House of Israel. There seem to be no obstacles to the formation of a church, with all its paraphernalia: even the membership seems readily available.

When considering religious policy, it is more relevant to explore the relationship between the more 'established' churches, such as the Catholic and Anglican, and the Government. During the colonial era, the leaders of these churches were part of the white ruling group, while the Hindus and Muslims had little political power. Adult suffrage and numbers made the Indians a force to be reckoned with in the post-independence period and since they constitute almost the entire membership of the Hindu and Muslim religions their religious leaders assumed added importance. However, this leadership lacked experience of political confrontation and an external base of support. Unlike the Catholic and Anglican clergy, who could look for support and personal promotion outside Guyana, the Indian religions are essentially locally based and are therefore at the mercy of a Government which controls over 80 per cent of the economy. So, although the PNC has never been able to win appreciable support among rank and file Indians, skilful use of patronage has allowed it to be able to call upon the support of a section of their religious leadership which is still divided and seemingly ineffective as an opposition to the regime.

The Anglicans, Methodists and Presbyterians who entered the country during slavery saw their task as that of turning the heathen slaves and Amerindians into Christians and teaching them to accept their position in the general scheme of things. Of course, the Churches were not always in agreement with the planters and the clergy of some of the more radical ones such as the London Missionary Society, were critics of the slavery system and advocates of political rights for the Black people once slavery had ended. On the whole, however, the religious denominations worked to maintain the status quo. Catholics have been in Latin America and the Caribbean from the time of 'discovery' and by the mid-sixteenth century Bartolome de Las Casa was already applying his fiery rhetoric in defence of Amerindian rights. But it was not until Portuguese immigration grew in scale in the 1830s that Catholicism became important in Guyana. When Indian immigration began the Christians treated Hinduisn and Islam as forms of paganism and it was only gradually that they began proselytizing the Indians.

When the PPP presented its challenge to the ruling group in 1953 the religious elite did not shirk its duty. The *Catholic Standard* published what it called a 'Soviet Life Series' which portrayed the Soviet Union and communism in a fashion which would have been laughable had it not been propagated by serious men of God set upon misleading a population ignorant of such matters. The so-called 'Soviet Life Series' went so far as to claim that it was a crime to laugh in the Soviet Union. Again, in 1961, when the Jagan Government stated its intention to take over the school system, this was explained as but another step in the communist plot of mass brainwashing and the Christian Social Council responded with a mammoth demonstration.

The religious elite, particularly the Catholics, supported the UF and thus applauded the Sandys' Constitution and fell in with the PNC/UF coalition Government. This elite had no love or respect for the PNC or the Black masses who supported it. And although most of the congregations of these Churches were Black, right up to independence, their top positions were filled by white expatriates. In 1856, not ten years after the complete abolition of slavery, the Anglican Church had ordained Lambert Mackenzie, its first Black priest, but such was the ambivalence which greeted Mackenzie that he was forced to leave for Sierra Leone, where his ministry was exemplary. But although the Anglicans were more progressive than the Catholics the entire ruling group was united in its determination to hold on to all top positions. The better schools, which were controlled by the religious elite, the Catholics in particular, were the preserves of whites and near-whites. These people supported the Coalition Government because they had no choice and their own disrespect for the Africans lured them into a sense of false security, believing that Burnham would have been easily controlled by the leader of the UF, the Portuguese businessman Peter D'Aguiar.

If this elite had no love for the PNC the contrary was also true and by a similar sleight of hand which the churchmen had applauded when it removed Jagan, Burnham removed the UF and immediately lost the support of this religious elite. Furthermore, he had begun to make radical noises reminiscent of the PPP but these men could only mutter under their breaths: they had lost the moral authority to protest and, more to the point, they were part of the political process which believed in, constructed and worked for the implementation of the political equation outlined in Chapter 2. It was fortunate for these Churches that Guyanization was removing these men from positions of authority. In 1970, the first Guyanese Bishop, Benedict Singh, was given charge of the Catholic Church and a similar process followed in the Anglican Church when Randolph George became Bishop.

The international environment was radicalized in the late 1960s and early 1970s. The decolonization process; the mass protests of minorities in the United States and other countries; the fervent search by the new states for forms of organization which would release them from the poverty left by the colonizers; the example of Cuba as a progressive state which seemed to be improving the life opportunities of its people; the growth of pop music and its spread to integrate people across different borders and cultures—all helped to create a new liberalism. The new churchmen were therefore more broadminded ideologically and were not caught in the moral dilemma of their predecessors. This was an ideological advantage for the PNC but it was also problematic. When that party began to talk about Marxism no 'Soviet Life Series' was organized against it but even so, when, in 1975, the Government was about to take over Church schools and anti-socialist murmurings were discerned, so aware was the PNC of the potential of the Church to make trouble that Burnham was forced to make one of his rare forays into the relationship between religion and politics. 'Ours', he reminded them, 'is a secular state in which there is, and can be, no established Church with special rights and privileges. But every Guyanese is free to, and will always continue to be free to, worship or not to worship, to believe or not to believe, without interference.' (Burnham, 1975, p. 18). With his sights set upon the Catholics and Anglicans, he reminded them of the segregation, discrimination and class bias which formed part of their not-too-distant history: 'But we do not blame their religion for their misdeeds'.

Again, we come upon that ironic streak which is easily found in Guyanese history. The very Churches which had supported constitutional and electoral manipulations were now—staffed by new men—beginning to protest against them. The PNC would argue that at the bottom of much of the anti-PNC rhetoric, and that of the Catholic Church in particular, there is still a chronic racism. Perhaps this is true but this contention does not alter the fact that there are legitimate reasons for protest. The Guyana Council of Churches provides an umbrella organization through which the different denominations discuss and take positions on important social issues. Not unlike its control of the TUC, the regime has used its control of some of the smaller churches to prevent the Council from opposing it too blatantly. By the late 1970s, however, the social crisis had reached such a level that the new men of the larger Churches had begun to make their voices heard. One of the Council's first acts of opposition to the regime was its condemnation of the 1978 referendum. This process has continued and as late as March 1985 the regime and sections of the Guyana Council of Churches were at loggerheads when the staff of the Council prepared a working paper to be discussed at its Annual General Meeting which claimed that the Government was in power by fraud and blamed it for the state of the economy. The AGM had to be postponed as supporters of the regime succeeded in preventing delegates, including Bishop Randolph George, from attending the meeting.

The PNC finds support among the leadership of the many smaller Christian Churches. These Churches tend to have members who are much more religiously active and who tend to look upon the Anglicans and Catholics as having strayed from the correct path. Many of their headquarters are in the United States, with large Black memberships who tend to be sympathetic towards Black leadership in the Third World, in addition to which the PNC has fostered a progressive external image. Party officials and Government ministers regularly climb the pulpits of these churches. One such favoured organization was the People's Temple of the late infamous Reverend Jim Jones. The mass suicide which took place at Jonestown, Guyana in November 1978 shocked the world but the Guyana Government, which must have given permission for the organization of the settlement in Guyana and allowed the Reverend Jones almost unlimited autonomy, claimed that since the vast majority of those who died were American citizens the disaster had little to do with Guyana. It has refused repeated opposition requests for an enquiry into the event and there have been serious suggestions that some senior members of the regime received favours from the Temple.

At present, another religious group, the House of Israel, is giving cause for concern. The House is headed by one Rabbi Washington, an American citizen wanted on charges of corporate blackmail in his own country. The Rabbi preaches a radical Black nationalism and his organization is estimated to have a membership of about 8,000 and its own guards, called 'royal cadets', of about 300. The Rabbi is a fervent supporter of the PNC and one of his brethren is said to have been responsible for stabbing to death a Catholic priest, Father Bernard Darke, on 11 July 1979, when the priest, who worked as a photographer for the *Catholic Standard* was taking photographs of a demonstration called to protest at the arrest of some WPA activists who were accused of setting fire to the building which housed the Office of the General Secretary of the PNC and the Ministry of National Development. Someone has been charged with the killing but the case drags on. More recently, members of the House of Israel were also reported to have been instrumental in preventing delegates from entering the 1985 AGM of the Council of Churches.

Military

Listening to opponents of the PNC, one gets the distinct impression that the only reason for the military build-up which has so obviously taken place is the PNC's intention to use the military to cow the masses, rig elections and suppress its more active opponents. However, in common with so much of what the PNC does, its military programme was developed in response to a genuine threat and real fears concerning Guyana's borders. In both areas the Government has had to carry out military operations to secure national territory. In January 1969 some ranchers in the Rupununi started an insurrection aimed at seizing a section of territory: it was quelled by the Guyana Defence Force (GDF). In a note handed to the Venezuelan Chargé d'Affaires in Georgetown on 8 January 1969, Acting Prime Minister,

Dr Ptolomy Reid, accused the Venezuelans of supplying arms and giving other aid to the rebels. The note claimed that the rebels were brought back to Guyana from Venezuelan training camps in Venezuelan aircraft and that one of the leaders of the rebellion, Ms Valerie Hart, was allowed to make an appeal for aid on Venezuelan radio. The regime believes that Venezuela encouraged the ranchers to take the action. There was also the Venezuelan occupation of the Guyana half of the border island of Ankoko. In August 1969, on the eastern border with Surinam, the GDF had to expel some Surinamese soldiers from the New River area and it claimed to have found information which led it to believe that the Surinamese had a plan to occupy the entire disputed area (*The New Road*, 1975, p. 34). Table 12 shows how military spending has greatly increased but we maintain that this must largely be seen against the background of the territorial troubles. This is not to deny that the regime uses the military in the fashion outlined by the opposition: indeed, as we will see presently, the leadership of the PNC has made every effort to divert the military from its responsibility in protecting the nation to that of supporting the leadership of the PNC.

The GDF came into being in 1965 as the national army of Guyana and its present role is said to be the maintenance of law and order and the territorial integrity of the country and to make contributions to the development effort. Up to 1969 the GDF was led by Colonel Ronald Pope, who was seconded from the British Army and it operated according to British military ethics, which hold that the Army should be loyal to the 'government of the day' and not be otherwise involved in politics. The result of the 1968 election was highly questionable and the validity of PNC rule was therefore in doubt. The army had good reason to remove it from office, so a new relationship had to be worked out which transferred the loyalty of the army from the nation to a part of the nation as represented by the PNC. Pope's departure opened the way for just such a formulation.

The concept of the 'People's Army' was coined to allow this shift of responsibility to take place. Burnham argued, rightly in our view, that Guyana needed an Army to protect itself but that she could not afford to keep one of the conventional type which sat in its barracks and waited for emergencies to arise. Another reason for having the Army kept busy with development projects was that the mutiny of the Trinidad and Tobago Regiment in 1970 had indicated quite clearly that the devil will find work for idle hands and, given the PNC's position, there was plenty to keep the GDF busy. Military service is voluntary and the GDF now has about 7,000 members organized in about twenty corps, ranging from the training and intelligence corps to the catering and band corps. It also has infantry, engineer, marine and air command units. The force, like all the paramilitary organizations, is still very much involved in developmental work in the fields of agriculture, mining, fishing, construction, etc.

The rationale for demanding that the GDF should support the PNC is unsound and since it provides the basis for similar support from the other security forces it deserves our attention. It was argued that; 'unless the army understood what the government was trying to do and sought to participate fully in its programme, there was bound to be collision between the government and the army.' Such reactionary ideas as '"Neutralism"—the feeling that soldiers should be free to embrace any sort of political philosophy and like mercenaries, be ready to serve any body, group or government, refusing to commit themselves to the party ideology that was supported by the broad masses of the Guyanese people' (ibid., p. 40) had to be changed and the army become committed to the PNC Government.

The logical and historical inconsistencies of this statement are so numerous that comment is unnecessary. It suffices to ask how the Army would decide which party, group or government has the support of the 'broad masses of the Guyanese people' and whether neutralism means that soldiers have the right to 'embrace any sort of political philosophy', or does it mean that, irrespective of what political philosophy they embrace as individuals, as soldiers their duty is to protect the constitutional democratic right of the people to be ruled by a government of their own choice?

By the end of 1973 all independent commentators agreed that the GDF was actively involved in suppressing the constitutional rights which they were empowered to uphold. After the election of that year, the *Catholic Standard* wrote: 'In the circumstances, the failure to seal boxes, the harassment of election personnel of the other parties who tried to follow the boxes, the wholly inexplicable detention of the boxes in the Guyana Defence Force compound for long periods—all these circumstances were bound to attract suspicion', and the *Caribbean Contact* of August 1973 concluded 'There is the clearest evidence of massive irregularities, including the seizure, impounding and tampering with ballot boxes, all of which were calculated to ensure that elections were neither free nor fair.' (Jagan, 1973, pp. 84–90). But the GDF, now committed to the PNC, saw the situation differently:

National elections were scheduled for July 1973. Realising that their hold on the electorate was slipping further and in an abortive attempt to forestall an obvious and overwhelming PNC victory, a campaign of violence and resistance was planned by the PPP. The GDF was called to aid the Civil power and prevented a break down of law and order that was planned by the gangsters. The operation established the maturity and competence of the Force. [*The New Road*, 1975, pp. 43–4.]

We have already considered the Guyana National Service. In 1976 the People's Militia was created, at a time of alert on the Venezuelan border. It is a voluntary force whose members continue their normal occupation until any outbreak of hostilities, when they are expected to defend their communities and assist the regular forces. The idea is to create a broad-based people's force with two classes of persons: those young enough to be trained to carry out strenuous operations and those who are to perform the functions usually left to home guards. It is hoped that each unit of the Militia will be autonomous and flexible enough to be self-supporting in times of emergency. The view that opposition forces hold of the Militia is similar to that which they hold of the other sections of the military.

Foreign policy

At each Congress of the ruling party between 1974 and 1983 Burnham maintained that the foreign policy of his party was an extension of its domestic policy and, seeming to attempt a logical fallacy, at the 1975 Congress he claimed that since the party had been following a progressive foreign policy its internal policy must also be progressive. 'Guyana' he claimed, led by the Vanguard Party, the People's National Congress, plays some small, but not unimportant role on the international stage, our members must feel some sense of pride. They [the membership] must remark that our foreign policy is a logical extension of our domestic policy and they must recognise that obviously our line has a great deal to commend it. [Burnham, 1975, p. 32.]

Many of the regime's staunchest critics will agree that the PNC has a progressive foreign policy and they will also agree that there is a link between its domestic and foreign policies. They will claim, however, that a progressive foreign policy is a necessary condition if a repressive regime is to maintain a progressive external image.

The foreign policy of the PNC has four main facets: non-alignment, Caribbean unity, support for the peoples of southern Africa in their struggle against racism and the protection of Guyana's borders. At his party's 1983 Congress, Burnham drew attention to his 1961 statement that Guyana would be a pawn of neither East nor West. Non-alignment was developed by President Tito of Yugoslavia after his rejection by Stalin and the Comintern and while he was still distrustful of the Western allies who had made a wartime agreement to share influence in Yugoslavia with the Russians. Burnham admired Tito's independent stand and, as it turned out, non-alignment fitted well into the context in which the PNC found itself. The party had come to power with the implicit or explicit aid of the CIA: it could not tempt fate by attempting to make alliances with the communist world. The closest it could venture was Yugoslavia, which was considered 'revisionist'. On the other hand, even if it wanted to—and there is no evidence that it did—it could not fall in with the West and still hope to be considered progressive. Developed in an atmosphere of uncertainty, non-alignment is a most flexible doctrine and the movement it spawned allows the greatest possible ideological maneouvrability. The PNC has adhered to it assiduously. It became a member of the movement's co-ordinating bureau and in 1972 had the cachet of holding the first major meeting of the movement in the Caribbean and Latin America, when the Conference of the Foreign Ministers of the Non-Aligned Countries was held in Georgetown.

The flexibility of non-alignment made it possible for Burnham to follow his personal preference for relations with China once American influence on that country had eased. In October 1971 the People's

Republic took its seat in the United Nations and began a series of diplomatic relationships. In April 1972 China agreed to make a G$52m. soft loan to Guyana for the construction of the country's first textile plant and in June 1972 diplomatic relations were established between the two countries, with the People's Republic establishing one of its first embassies in Latin America and the Caribbean in Guyana. It may be useful to note that although diplomatic relations were established with the Soviet Union in 1970, that country was not then allowed to open an embassy in Guyana. Relations between these two countries have remained good. The relationship with China also helped the PNC's socialist image at a time when association with Yugoslavia alone would have certainly reinforced the belief that co-operativism was revisionist. In the late 1960s and early 1970s it was difficult to find a country more radical than China, which was challenging the Soviet Union for the leadership of world communism.

With non-alignment, the PNC was able to bide its time until the international environment allowed it to form closer relations with the communist world, led by the Soviet Union. Although it began diplomatic relations with the Soviet Union in December 1970, to do so with Cuba would still have constituted a risk so it was not until 1972, together with the other major countries in the Commonwealth Caribbean, that diplomatic relations were opened with that country. In the mid-1970s the regime began to move closer to the communist world: this may have been hastened by threats of destablization as the Government began to take over the multinationals. In April 1975 Burnham visited Cuba where he was rewarded with the Jose Marti Award, Cuba's second highest honour. In December 1975 the Barbados' Government succumbed to American pressure and withdrew refuelling facilities from the Cubans on their way to Angola. Trinidad and Tobago also refused, but in early 1976 the Guyana regime accommodated the Cubans in the face of similar American pressure. In the mid-1970s there were high expectations that the PNC and PPP would, at the least, develop a working relationship. The PPP had adopted 'critical support' and after years of distancing themselves from each other Jagan and Burnham shared the same platform at the 1976 May Day rally. But all hopes were dashed as the United States began to make destabilizing noises and the regime was unwilling to risk the equation outlined in

Chapter 2. However, over two dozen Marxist parties and groups attended the 1981 Congress of the PNC; they ranged from the communist parties of the Soviet Union, China, Cuba and most of Eastern Europe to the Polisario Front, the Solidarity Committee of Chile, the New Jewel Movement of Grenada and the Sandinista Front of Nicaragua.

The massive economic difficulties which it now faces and the reluctance of the Reagan administration to come to its assistance unless it makes major programmatic reversals is forcing the PNC to make new overtures to the PPP, hoping that this will panic the United States into aiding it or result in economic assistance from the communist world. However, the Reagan administration seems determined to call the regime's bluff and the Soviets and their partners are distrustful of the PNC and will not deal with it seriously until it makes major and lasting concessions to the PPP.

The Government recognizes these difficulties and so has brought to the fore an approach which provides it with an alternative international economic strategy and which could be worked out within the Non-aligned Movement. At the Commonwealth Heads of Government Conference held in Kingston Jamaica in 1975 Burnham was one of the chief advocates of the New International Economic Order. However, since it has become patently clear that the West is unlikely to allow any major changes to the world monetary and trading systems, in 1983 Burnham concluded that: 'The immediate need is for a South–South dialogue. . . . there is no advantage to be gained from complaining about the unreal, immoral distribution of the world's wealth.' (Burnham, 1983, p. 6). Collective self-reliance at both the regional and international levels is one of three focuses of the PNC's international economic policy.

Since its formation, the PNC has consistently associated itself with Caribbean unity. Apart from a genuine wish to see a united West Indies, the party was supported mainly by Africans who were in the minority in Guyana but in the majority in the West Indies. On the other hand, the PPP received the major part of its support from Indians had to be careful on the issue of federation, particularly since the NLF was propagating an anti-federalist line among the Indians in the rural areas. In 1956, explaining why he was forced to criticize the 'ultra left' of the PPP, which consisted of Rory Westmaas, Martin Carter, Lionel Jeffrey and others, Jagan stated that: 'Secondly, and more fundamentally, this small group advocated the abandonment of the party's stand on the West Indian Federation and urged unconditional support for it' (Jagan, 1966, p. 176). He continued to argue that such a position was adventurist since it failed to take into consideration 'the views and weaknesses of the rank and file' (ibid.).

The West Indian Federation dissolved in 1962 but once the PNC took office in 1964 it began to take an energetic interest in Caribbean unity. In 1967 Antigua, Barbados and Guyana were the original signatories to the document which established the Caribbean Free Trade Area which, on 4 July 1973, became the Caribbean Community and Common Market, consisting of Antigua, Barbados, Belize, Dominica, Grenada, Guyana, Jamaica, Montserrat, St Kitts/Nevis, Saint Lucia, St. Vincent and the Grenadines and Trinidad and Tobago. By the late 1970s the economic situation of member countries, particularly Guyana and Jamaica, forced them to take protectionist measures which greatly strained their relationship. Difficulties arose in applying the Community's rules of origin which attempt to verify genuine regional products from those which are imported; the Multilateral Clearing Facility collapsed after its credit limit of US$100m. was exceeded. In 1983 Guyana owed US$98m., including US$65m. to Barbados and the debts were reordered on a bilateral basis. Inter-regional trade fell by 13 per cent in 1983. The Marxist rhetoric of the PNC and the coming to power by revolution on 13 March 1979 of the New Jewel Movement in Grenada, which then refused to hold parliamentary elections as was being demanded by the more conservative members in the group did nothing to improve the situation. In 1981 the Movement for Caribbean Unity had reached its lowest point. Although the Council of Ministers of Trade met regularly to monitor the Common Market agreements and deal with the growing number of complaints, a Caricom Heads of Governments Meeting had not been held for five years.

However, in 1982 a Summit was held in Jamaica and one has been held every year since. In 1983 agricultural ministers re-emphasized the need for the regional food and nutrition strategy which was approved in 1982 and is intended to improve the standard of nutrition, increase agricultural production and establish food reserves mainly through the

Caribbean Food Corporation which attracts investments for agriculture and food marketing projects. The ministers approved nineteen projects to be implemented by 1985, which should be of some benefit to the Guyana Government which believes that its country has the potential to become the breadbasket of the Community. The production difficulties outlined above make such an aspiration extremely problematical, however. The 1984 Heads of Government Meeting agreed to seek external finance to revive the Multilateral Clearing Facility but the Prime Ministers of Dominica—Ms Eugenia Charles—and Jamaica—Mr Edward Seaga—who were the main supporters of the American invasion of Grenada in October 1983, were supporting a change of rules which could exclude Guyana from the Community. Ms Charles even voiced the opinion that Guyana was not really a Caribbean country.

Quite apart from a genuine wish to support progressive movements around the world (which has been limited by the operational context of the regime), the racial composition of the PNC's leadership and the vast majority of its supporters render the situation in southern Africa particularly offensive to the regime and it has consistently supported the liberation movements in that area. As we have seen, it provided support for the Cuban airlift to Angola. At the Non-Aligned Foreign Ministers meeting held in Georgetown in 1972 Guyana was given responsibility for helping Zambia implement the commitment of the movement to assist all liberation organizations in southern Africa, including Namibia, and in 1974 Guyana became the President of the Council of Namibia. In his address to the International Forum on the Liberation of Southern Africa which was held in Georgetown in 1981, Burnham restated his uncompromising position towards apartheid. 'It is incumbent upon us all in the circumstances, even at the cost of sacrifice, to render all assistance to our brothers in Namibia and South Africa struggling to be free, for their cause is our cause, their victory will be our victory.' (Burnham, 1981, p. 7).

With regard to the border disputes, the Government uses its influence at all international levels to frustrate its opponents' position. At both the 7th Conference of Heads of Governments of the Non-Aligned Countries which was held in Delhi in March 1983 and at the Conference of the Heads of Governments of the Caribbean

Community held in 1983 Guyana received support for its position. The Conferences called upon Venezuela to desist from actions likely to affect the economic development of Guyana and urged the parties to search for a peaceful settlement to the dispute.

10 Guyana: Beyond Burnham

Colonialism had left Guyana in a state of confusion that was extra-ordinary even by its own standards. The economy was lopsided, the political structure had been allowed to disintegrate and was then stuck together by a formula which gave rise to the political equation which has underlain this entire analysis, and the people, divided at one level, were united in the greater expectations they nurtured of the post-independence period. At one period the Indians appeared the political losers but as economic conditions worsened, it became clear that, at best, the colonial solution only benefited international capital. We say at best because even this became uncertain.

The years between the formation of the PNC and the death of Burnham saw that party deteriorate from a genuine forum of discussion, even if primarily of one racial group, into an organ through which the leadership manipulates a section of the population for its own survival. The party Constitution demonstrates that it is not a democratic arrangement and the new President, who drafted these rules in his position as legal adviser to the party, is unlikely to divest himself of their protection.

We have maintained that the leadership of the PNC introduced the 1980 national Constitution not only to fulfil its ambition for added trappings of office but because it genuinely wanted to institutionalize certain socialist aspirations. It is certainly true that the many un-employed to whom this constitution guarantees a right to work have no legal redress against the authorities but it is perhaps unrealistic to believe that this could have been allowed in a country at Guyana's level of development and with its many problems. Burnham has not lived to see the socialism he promised to build within 'our' lifetime but with the 1980 Constitution he has left his successors with an albatross around their necks should they decide upon a volte-face.

The major problem now facing the new leadership is how to deal with the growing trade union militancy, given that new elections are due in the first half of 1986. It is usual for a break in leadership to offer opportunities for new initiatives but whether this could occur in this situation is doubtful. Those who now control the state were as belligerent towards the unions as was Burnham and although it would be tempting to use Burnham's absence to introduce a new *rapprochement* with the unions this cannot be done immediately without tarnishing Burnham's image and to do so would be extremely dangerous. The new President and Leader of the PNC has little public support and the regime is very unpopular so, at least for the time being, it must depend upon the Burnham tradition to maintain some legitimacy. Therefore, in the near future, we are likely to see policies which are intended to bolster rather than detract from Burnham's image and this will not help to ease the problems with the trade unions.

One question many people will ask is whether or not elections will be banned now that the restraining hand of Burnham has been removed. We think not. Central to the equation (though by no means an inevitable feature of it) which this new leadership is also committed to maintain is that the threat of peaceful political take-over by Marxists must be ever present.

The reader will be excused for concluding that we are about to leave the object of our discussion in as hopeless a state as we found it for we have held out no hope of change in the near future. The PNC's claim to be constructing socialism is in direct contradiction to its perennial struggle to maintain the equation outlined in the second chapter of this book. Either that or it has a peculiar conception of socialism. It may be possible for any group of people within a society to overthrow capitalism but the construction of socialism, outside this initial stage, must be effected by the working people themselves. Socialism cannot be handed down: it is praxis, i.e. the process whereby conscious human self-motivated activity gradually facilitates the development of the best individual and social potentials. Within the context of Guyana, national unity is a *sine qua non* of such self-motivated activity. However, that cannot be achieved without the regime being willing to make real concessions to opposition forces and real concessions cannot be made without endangering the status quo. In recent months there have been discussions between the PNC and PPP intended to create the conditions for national unity, and as this volume goes to press more comprehensive discussions are planned. It is difficult to see how after over two decades of claiming that free and fair elections within a multiparty system are of primary importance, the PPP could accept terms which do not fulfil these aspirations without losing all credibility and it is even more incredible to think that the PNC would offer such terms, thus destroying itself. It appears that the ideological objective of the regime is a non-starter.

So far we have attempted, as much as is possible within the context we have described, to avoid an over-reliance on personalities. However, any assessment of the future of Guyanese society must depend upon how the current actors manipulate the scenario outlined in these pages and as the reader is unfamiliar with these 'new men' we will proceed to discuss possible policy responses as the alternatives which they must confront are outlined.

Firstly, the new leaders may choose to maintain the equation with a capitalist ethos. Writers continue to emphasize the relationship between democracy and development but at the same time it should be remembered that economic growth has taken place under the generals in Brazil, the dominant party situation in Mexico, in the Philippines under Marcos, in North and South Korea, in the People's Republic of China, etc.: that is, under diverse governmental arrangements which many would not consider to be democratic. By unleashing and foster- ing the individual propensity to struggle for, and accumulate, material goods the regime may short-circuit the problems of national disunity and pull the country out of its economic troubles. However, even if it is not universally true that a significant degree of democracy is neces- sarily essential to economic growth, we must remember that in Guyana the undemocratic nature of the equation does express itself in specific ways which have direct and indirect negative consequences for development.

As we have seen, the political struggle between the PPP and the PNC has an economic cost which the country can ill afford but those who demand increased democratic participation in Guyana believe it to be essential for rebuilding the confidence of the people. The disillusion- ment which now pervades Guyanese society is suggestive of the fact that many people have voted with their feet and a much larger section conceives of their salvation in activities which run counter to government programmes in which they have no faith. In their usual roundabout manner the regime accepts that much dissatisfaction exists. Thus, the General Secretary of the PNC, recognizing that times were bad and that many people were disillusioned, felt obliged to end his address to the 1983 Congress with the following words: 'Be steadfast, in season and out of season.' (*General Secretary's Address*, 1983, p. 35).

The current political situation gives rise to contradictions which increase this disillusionment. For example, the Government is never tired of propounding the virtues of, and its beliefs in, democracy. It has even constitutionalized it. But everyone is aware that political democracy is non-existent and, for fear of handing more power to its opponents, the regime must think twice before introducing industrial democracy. Furthermore, although the opposition has no realistic chance of gaining power legitimately, it is still able to articulate grievances in these and other areas, thus adding to the frustration.

But although part of the blame for the general malaise, helplessness and the resultant low production can be placed upon the direct operations of the equation, there is an important area which has to do not with the equation as such, but with the manner in which it is made to operate under the present leadership of the PNC. A few examples will illustrate the point.

Early in the 1970s the Government banned or severely restricted the importation of certain consumer items. After much public dissatisfaction, people came to accept the argument that local substitutes should be used where possible to save foreign exchange for development purposes. Flushed with this 'victory' but also compelled by economic difficulties, by 1980 the Government had removed almost every desirable consumer item from the shelves and even basic necessities were difficult to find. Quite apart from the fact that, rightly or wrongly, many people did not believe that their leaders were making the sacrifices they were demanding of the population, the planners failed to realize that such a programme must take into consideration the culture and aspirations of the people. The majority of Guyanese had aspirations, for which they were willing to work and sacrifice, aspirations which went far beyond acquiring the basic necessities. By relentlessly chipping away at what was available to fulfil these desires, the regime has severely reduced the people's desire to work.

Secondly, throughout the world, and Guyana is no exception,

people have sacrificed to provide their children with an education which they hope will give them self-fulfillment and lucrative and less alienating work. Forced to cut large numbers of people from the bureaucracy and having nowhere to send them but to cut sugar cane, the regime sought to make this universal aspiration into something of a moral crime. People whose parents had gone through much deprivation to give them an education and had themselves worked hard to avoid such tasks as cane cutting were told, by people who themselves held their positions as a result of training under the colonial system, that that system had trained them in irrelevant skills which were now useless. However, the regime did not offer retraining in comparable skills. Without a word of consolation, it rudely sent these people to do the very work they had sought to avoid. These people were well aware that those in neighbouring countries who had gone through a similar education process, and relatives who had emigrated, were not treated in this way. This is not meant to imply that the classical bias of the British colonial education system is not a difficulty which ex-colonies must overcome, but we do question a method which negates whole sections of the population and destroys all their expectations almost at a stroke.

Thirdly, Guyana does not make the best of its fishing resources which would certainly have helped those parts of the country which, notwithstanding the bravado of the regime, find it difficult to acquire an adequate supply of protein. The Government answer is that fresh fish is more nutritious than canned and so it has proceeded to do nothing. Whether it is always convenient to use fresh food is either not considered or thought irrelevant. This, of course, must be added to its whole attitude in relation to the needs of the population.

The regime is paternalistic: it knows what is best. It propounds a variety of sanitized positions which, even if true in ideal terms, bear no relation to the real life, customs and aspirations of the people. As we have seen, when emergency measures had to be taken, the people were not provided with sensible explanations but with a hodgepodge of ideological absurdities. The Government does not even have to act as a government since it has disfranchized the population. This is why democratic accountability seems to provide one answer to the problems now facing Guyana. It is one method of preventing an autocratic government from trampling upon dreams and expectations and of providing an environment in which people will be willing to work and make sacrifices.

However, it must be evident that while the status quo allows the present leadership of the PNC to behave as it does, that behaviour has been dictated not by the political context but by a defective social and philosophical perspective. Another socialist or, indeed, capitalist orientated leadership would have acted differently, making certain that policies were much more attuned to the preferences of their citizens, allowing freer expression in consumption, production and other social activities and providing more sensible explanations for policy decisions. Under the present leadership of the PNC self-expression is curtailed in all spheres, leaving the people with the alternative of physically or mentally leaving its purview. Chapter 4 shows how no mechanism exists, even within the party, which could compel the top leaders to act at the cost of their jobs. Where the majority of the economy is in the hands of such people this is dangerous. In communist countries the political bureaux and central committees constitute serious checks on performance.

International capital must be aware, as we are, that it need not risk the equation by attempting to remove the PNC from government; although, after fruitless years of working with the leadership of the party before Burnham's death, the removal of the leadership must have been under serious consideration, not only, or even primarily because of its socialist orientation, but because it has become an embarrassment and is endangering the very system it is supposed to protect. It is presiding over a steadily crumbling economy and rising social unrest which could result in revolution. However, if the new leadership switches its support to a capitalist orientation and is successful in privatizing the economy, it will most likely be forced to consider the multifarious interests of a free enterprise society, thus avoiding both the dogmatism of its predecessor and the problems of accountability for the economy which have led to stagnation and decline. On the other hand, individual self-interest may serve to weaken the impact of party politics upon economic development. It is when we consider the three major actors: President Hoyte, First Vice-President and Prime Minister Hamilton Green and Deputy Leader Ptolomy Reid, that the policy just outlined becomes a distinct possibility.

Hoyte is perhaps the most vociferous protector of the equation we have been discussing but he is not known for a strong commitment to socialism. Educated as a lawyer in London, Hoyte worked for the same legal firm as Burnham and has been in every Guyanese government since 1968. He is relatively young (being 56 years old when he became President) but his health is poor. His major drawback is that he lacks popular support even among the remaining supporters of the PNC and this cannot be taken lightly in a small country where leadership has been very personal. It is Hoyte who, over the last decade, has been responsible for economic management in Guyana and, as we have seen, this period has been one of steady decline. His ability to pull Guyana out of its present problems must therefore be in serious doubt but since he will be aware of this, it is likely that he will make economic recovery a priority not only to rectify a somewhat tarnished reputation but also to provide foundations on which to build his popularity.

Recovery will be extremely difficult if the status quo is to be maintained and serious concessions are not made to the PPP. So, since Hoyte is more technocratic than ideological and guards the equation with his life, we can probably expect the discussions with the PPP to gradually wither away and major concessions to be made to international capital hoping that the latter will provide the resources which the economy badly needs if it is to take off. Hoyte is not disliked by the United States but after its experience with Burnham the United States will demand a more stringent commitment to free enterprise for any aid they provide. But even in dealing with this source, the new President will have to face a serious problem. Over the years it is he who has constantly been responsible for whittling away the people's standard of living, so if he intends to build a popular base he will have to be cautious in accepting any financial package which could lead to a further cut in living standards.

One must understand that the leadership of the PNC is unlikely to fight among itself if the seniority which existed under Burnham is maintained. It will take some considerable time before Hoyte will risk removing any of the other two actors without their consent. Indeed, it is the other two who have greater public support and he will need them to lend credibility to his regime. In the new Prime Minister he will have an ideological ally. Green, who is five years younger than Hoyte, made his name as a party activist in the bloody days of the 1960s, and try as he may to create a more respectable political image, that reputation has stayed with him. Somewhat unfairly, he is considered to be anti-intellectual and anti-socialist, but someone who can get things done. He leaves the impression of being tough, a quality which the population, seeing society crumbling about it, appears to believe is the answer to the country's problems. However, this quality is likely to add an unsavoury aroma to the regime for, since Green is the new President's main competitor, we can expect the development of a contest to see who is stronger and this could have negative repercussions on the society. Where Hoyte and Green are likely to part company is on the need to maintain the equation outlined above. The latter is likely to consider it a humbug while Hoyte is committed to it. That said, Green is a useful person with whom Hoyte could leave economic management, knowing that there will be some support for that move while at the same time saving himself from any embarrassment in the event of other failures.

Of course, the leadership could opt for the democratic socialist alternative but this would mean that it would have to be willing to risk the equation. If properly organized and supported in both its institutional and ideological forms, the co-operative schema could introduce the environment of mass democratic support which is necessary to stimulate initiative and development but it could also be terminal for conventional political relations as workers and citizens come to govern themselves without the mediation of political parties (Markovic, 1982). In terms of personalities, the Deputy Leader of the Party, Dr Ptolomy Reid, is the socialists' most certain ally amongst this group. He has some support among grass-roots PNC supporters but is considered too dogmatic by the middle class, who see him as the main architect of the policy which removed foreign imports from the shops. However, there is no indication that he will be willing to lead such a faction; quite the contrary. He is older than Burnham was when he died, was removed from the positions of Prime Minister and General Secretary of the party in 1984 and has shown no inclination to return to the political fray.

But so far we have only been discussing personalities. The PNC has been in office for over two decades and, together with the other opposition parties, has created a socialist consciousness among the population which cannot be easily eradicated. Even among Guyanese capitalists, rarely does one find the propagation of views which are devoid of any socialist persuasion. Every member of the PNC's CEC has committed him/herself to radical socialism at one time or another. The General Secretary of the Party is, after all, Chandisingh, a committed Marxist who crossed the floor from the PPP, and although the position of General Secretary is not as important as in most communist countries, it cannot be dismissed. The best bet for those of socialist persuasion within the party would seem to be to try to maintain some form of collective leadership, knowing full well that they have the entire ethos of the party and even the national constitution behind them.

We have been discussing changes as they are likely to occur mainly within the PNC but many people would like to see that party removed from office and will be considering what the chances of this are, now that Burnham has left the scene. Although the military appears totally submerged under the ideological supremacy of the PNC, it still has to be considered. Hamilton Green is the leader with the greatest support and contact within the military and so long as he remains relatively happy the military is likely to stay in its barracks. Of course this is our opinion too. Like everywhere else, there are those in the military who believe that things have become unstuck and cannot be rectified by the PNC and these young men may well believe that the time to act is now. However, if by the time this book reaches the shelves the military has not acted, we doubt whether it is likely to do so for the time being.

The PPP and the WPA are waiting in the sidelines but we do not place high priority on their coming to power. We have already said a great deal about the PPP and since it is more or less reluctant to organize an armed opposition to the regime we can expect it to remain in its traditional position. As for the WPA, it has modified its Marxism to make itself more acceptable to internal and external capital. Its hope is that, faced with rising unrest, the PNC will run aground and it will pick up the pieces with the support of international capital which will see it as a better alternative to the PPP. While this may be possible, it is extremely improbable that under conditions of internal turmoil the

WPA would ever be able to come to power without some concessions to the PPP and that would mean the withdrawal of American support.

The sort of situation we have been considering in this conclusion is made for stagnation and decline. In the near future the top leaders of the PNC will be signalling left but wanting to turn right, only to find the road to the right blocked by the historical ideological position to which they have committed themselves. The two orientations will have to co-exist in the PNC for some considerable time. The question is what will happen to the Guyanese people in the meantime? We are not hopeful.

Bibliography

Able, Christopher (1983), 'Documentary Review', *Journal of Latin American Studies*, **15**, p. 2.

Adamson, Jack A. and Holland, Harold (1969), *The Shepherd of the Ocean*, Boston, Gambit.

Annual Report of the Ministry of Co-operatives (1983), Georgetown, Ministry of Information.

Argument for Unity Against the Dictatorship in Guyana (1983), Georgetown, Working People's Alliance.

Bacchus, M. K. (1967), 'The Ministerial System at Work: A Case Study of Guyana, *Social and Economic Studies*, pp. 34–57, University of the West Indies.

Bank of Guyana Report (annually), Bank of Guyana, Georgetown.

The Boundary Question with British Guiana, now Guyana (1982), Caracas, Ministry of External Relations.

Brass, Paul (ed.) (1985), *Ethnic Groups and the State*, London, Croom Helm.

Budget, Georgetown, Ministry of Information.

Burnham, Forbes (1970a), *A Destiny to Mould*, Caribbean, Longman.

—— (1970b), 'A Vision of the Co-operative Republic' in L. Searwar (ed.), *Co-operative Republic: Guyana*, Georgetown, Ministry of Information.

—— (1974), *Declaration of Sophia*, Georgetown, Ministry of Information.

—— (1975), *Towards the Socialist Revolution*, Georgetown, Ministry of Information.

—— (1976), *Report to the Nation*, Georgetown, Ministry of Information.

—— (1977), *Economic Liberation Through Socialism*, Georgetown, Ministry of Information.

—— (1978), *Press Conference: The IMF Standby Arrangement*, Georgetown, Ministry of Information.

—— (1979), *Towards the People's Victory*, Georgetown, Ministry of Information.

—— (1980), *Of Human Rights*, Georgetown, Ministry of Information.

—— (1981), *The Struggle for Human Dignity*, Georgetown, Ministry of Information.

—— (1982), *Address to the First Session of the Supreme Congress of the People*, Georgetown, Ministry of Information.

—— (1983), *Will to Survive*, Georgetown, Ministry of Information.

Chandisingh, Ranji (1979), *Education in the Revolution*, Georgetown, Secretariat of the People's National Congress.

— (1976) *Why I Left the PPP*, Georgetown, Secretariat of the PNC.

Chase, Ashton, (1965) *A History of Trade Unionism in Guyana: 1900 to 1961*, Georgetown, New Guyana Company.

Child, Clifton J. (1950); 'The Venezuela-British Guiana Boundary Arbitration of 1899' *The American Journal of International Law*, 44 No. 4.

Collins, B. A. N. (1965) 'Acceding to Independence: Some Constitutional Problems of a Polyethnic Society (British Guiana)' *Civilization* no. 15, London.

Collymore, Clinton (1984), *Bitter Sugar and the Working People*, Georgetown, New Guyana Company.

Constitutional Commission: Report of the British Guiana (1954), London, HM Stationery Office.

Constitution of the Co-operative Republic of Guyana (1980), Georgetown, Ministry of Information.

Co-operativism: Policy Paper of the People's National Congress (1980), Georgetown, Secretariat of the PNC.

Daly, Vere T. (1970), 'Historical Background to the Co-operative Republic' in *Co-operative Republic: Guyana 1970* (ed.) L. Searwar.

Delson, Roberta Marx (1981), *Caribbean History and Economics*, London, Gordon and Breach Science Publishers.

Depres, Leo A. (1967), *Cultural Pluralism and Nationalist Politics in British Guiana*, Chicago, Rand McNally.

Documents of the 19th Congress (1976), Georgetown, People's Progressive Party.

Dowden, Rupert A. (1971), 'Glimpses of Co-operatives', *Daily Chronicle*, Georgetown.

Economic Survey of Latin America (1981), United Nations.

The Europa Year Book (1983 and 1984), London, Europa Publications.

The Food Crisis in Guyana, Georgetown, New Guyana Company.

For Socialism in Guyana (1982), Prague, Orbis Press Agency.

Forward with the Women's Struggle (1983), Georgetown, PPP.

Furnivall, J. S. (1939), *Netherlands India: A Study of Plural Economy*, Cambridge, Cambridge University Press.

General Secretary's Address (1983), Georgetown, Secretariat of the PNC.

General Secretary's Report (1984), Georgetown, Trade Union Congress.

Glasgow, Roy (1970), *Guyana: Race and Politics Between Africans and East Indians*, The Hague, Martinus Nijhoff.

Graham, Sara and Gordon, Derek (1977), *The Stratification System and Occupational Mobility in Guyana*, Kingston, Institute of Social and Economic Research, University of the West Indies.

Grant, Olga S. (1975), *History of the Co-operative Movement in Guyana*, George-town, Co-operative College.

Green, J. E. (1974), *Race vs. Politics in Guyana*, Kingston, Institute of Social and Economic Research, University of the West Indies.

Guyana: Crisis; Bankruptcy; Solution (1982), Georgetown, New Guyana Company.

Guyana: Fraudulent Revolution (1984), London, Latin American Bureau.

Guyana Information Bulletin, Georgetown, People's Progressive Party.

Guyana National Service: State Paper (1973), Georgetown, Ministry of Informa-tion.

Guyana Report: Midpoint of the UN Decade for Women (1981), Georgetown, Women's Affairs Bureau.

Handbook of International Trade and Development Statistics (1984), New York, United Nations.

Hoyte, Desmond (1980), *Local Democratic Organs*, Georgetown, Ministry of Information.

— (1981), *Action in Partnership*, Georgetown, Ministry of Information.

Hoyte, Desmond and Mohamed Shahabbuddeen (1979), *A Socialist Economy Through Agricultural, Industrial and Technical Development and The Constitu-tion: Philosophy and Mechanics*, Georgetown, Secretariat of the PNC.

Human Rights Violations in Guyana (1982), Georgetown, New Guyana Company.

Investment Code: The Guyana (1979), Georgetown, Ministry of Information.

Jagan, Cheddi (1966), *The West on Trial*, London, Michael Joseph.

Jagan, Cheddi and Karan, Ram (1974), *Race & Politics in Guyana*, Georgetown, New Guyana Company.

Jagan, Janet (1973), *Army Intervention in the 1973 Election in Guyana*, George-town, PPP.

Jeffrey, H. B. (1982), *Socialist Theory and Co-operatives: Guyana*, Georgetown, Co-operative College.

King, K. F. S. (1973), *A Great Future Together*, Georgetown, Ministry of Infor-mation.

Kurian, George T. (1982), *Encyclopedia of the Third World: Volume 2*, London, Mansell.

Kwayana, Eusi (*9 and 16 December 1960), Burnham and the Guianese Revolution*, Georgetown, *New Nation*.

— (1976), *Some Aspects of Pseudo-Socialism in Guyana*, Trinidad and Tobago, University of the West Indies.

— (November and December 1981), 'Guyana: The Second Republic', *Carib-bean Contact*, Bridgetown, Barbados.

Local Democratic Organs Act (1980), Georgetown, Ministry of Information.
Lloyds Bank Group: Economic Report: "Guyana" (1984), London.
Lutchman, Harold (1972), 'Race and Bureaucracy in Guyana', *Journal of Comparative Administration*.
McKenzie, H. I. (1967), 'The Plural Society Debate: Some Comments on a Recent Contribution', *Social and Economic Studies*, **15**.
Mandel, J. (1976), *Continuity and Change in Guyanese Underdevelopment, Monthly Review*, **128**.
Manley, Robert (1979), *Guyana Emergent*, Boston, G. K. Hall & Co.
Markovic, Mihailo (1982), *Democratic Socialism*, Sussex, The Harvester Press.
Marshall, A. H. (1955), *Report on Local Government in British Guiana*, London, HM Stationery Office.
Mirror: Overseas and Daily, Georgetown, New Guyana Company.
Newman, P. (1960), 'The Economic Future of British Guiana' *Social and Economic Studies*, **9**, University of the West Indies.
The New Road (1975), Georgetown, Guyana Defence Force.
O'Loughlin, Carleen (1959), 'The Economy of British Guyana: A National Accounts Study', *Social and Economic Studies*, University of the West Indies.
Population Census of Guyana, Georgetown.
Party Constitution (1974 and 1983), Georgetown, Secretariat of the PNC.
Paxton, John (1982 and 1983), *The Statesman's Year Book*, London, Macmillan.
Payne, H. W. L., *Co-operative Socialism Revisited* (1978), Georgetown, National Archives.
PPP Thunder (Burnhamite), 22 June 1957, Georgetown, National Archives.
— (1973), *History of the People's National Congress*, Georgetown, National Archives.
Project Report of the Women's Revolutionary Socialist Movement (1984), Georgetown, Secretariat of the PNC.
Referendum: A Question of Human Rights (1978), Georgetown, Committee of Concerned Citizens.
Report on the Fourth Biennial Congress (1981), Georgetown, Secretariat of the PNC.
Report on Guyana: Midpoint of the Decade for Women (1980), Georgetown, Ministry of Information.
Report of the Technical Committee of the Guyana Trades Union Congress, (1982), Georgetown, TUC.
Rodney, Walter, (1981), *A History of the Guyanese Working People: 1871–1905*, London, Heineman.
Rodran, H. (1966), 'Illegitimacy in the Caribbean Social Structure: A Reconsideration', *American Sociological Review*.

Roraima Journal (1977), Georgetown, Ministry of Information.

Schoenrich, Otto (1949), 'The Venezuela–British Guiana Boundary Dispute', *American Journal of International Law*, **43**, No. 3.

Second Development Plan (1972), Georgetown, Ministry of Information.

A Short Documentary History of the Political Developments of the People's National Congress (1975), Georgetown, National Archives.

Simms, Peter (1966), *Trouble in Guyana*, London, Allen & Unwin.

Smith, M. G. (1960), 'Social and Cultural Pluralism' in Vara Rubin (ed.), *Social and Cultural Pluralism in the Caribbean*, Annals of the New York Academy of Science.

—— (1974), *Plural Society in the British West Indies*, Berkeley, University of California Press.

Smith, R. T. (1956), *The Negro Family in British Guyana*, London, Routledge & Kegan Paul.

—— (1961), 'Review of Social and Cultural Pluralism in the Caribbean', *American Anthropologist*.

—— and Jayawardena, Chandra (1959), 'Marriage and the Family Among East Indians in British Guiana', *Social and Economic Studies*.

Smooha, Sammy (1975), 'Pluralism and Conflict: A Theoretical Explanation', *Plural Societies*, **VI**, No. 3.

Speakers Brief No. 4: Youth Development (1980), Georgetown, Secretariat of the PNC.

Standing, G. (1979), 'Socialism and Basic Needs in Guyana' in *Poverty and Basic Needs*, G. Standing and R. Szal (eds), Geneva, ILO.

Statistical Yearbook for Latin America (1983), New York, United Nations.

Szajkowski, B. (1982), *Establishment of Marxist Regimes*, London, Butterworth Scientific.

Thomas, Clive (1982), 'Guyana: The World Bank Group and the General Crisis' in *Social and Economic Studies*, **31** No. 4, University of the West Indies.

—— (1984), 'State Capitalism in Guyana: an Assessment of Burnham's Co-operative Socialist Republic' in F. Ambursley and R. Cohen (eds), *Crisis in the Caribbean*, London, Heinemann.

Van den Berghe, Pierre L. (1974), 'Pluralism' in John S. Honigmann (ed.) *Handbook of Social and Cultural Anthropology*, New York, Rand McNally.

Webber, A. R. F. (1931), *Centenary History of British Guiana*, Georgetown, The Argosy Company.

Wallerstein, Immanuel (1979), *The Capitalist World Economy*, Cambridge, Cambridge University Press.

Women's Affairs Bureau (1982), Georgetown, Women's Affairs Bureau.

Index